A Compilation
from

Warren Litzman
Watchman Nee
Gene Edwards

The SeedSowers
Christian Books Publishing House
Auburn, Maine 04212-3368

Part I is taken from a book by Warren Litzman entitled *The Shape of the Future Church.* Used by permission.
Part II is taken from the original and uncopyrighted edition of a book by Watchman Nee entitled *Concerning Our Missions.*
Published by:
The SeedSowers
Christian Books Publishing House
P.O. Box 3368
Auburn, Maine 04212-3368
ISBN 0-940232-47-2
Library of Congress Catalog Number 91-76171

# Dedication

To those who have ceased denominating themselves from other believers.

# Acknowledgement

The one person most responsible for the detail work on this book, and the one who worked so many hours on the manuscripts, bears special recognition here. I speak of my secretary, Denise Sirois.

# Contents


## Part I - Warren Litzman

1 The Shape of the Future Church ... 1
2 Daring Is Needed for the Future Church ... 5
3 A Loss of the Centrality of Christ ... 7
4 The Importance of Seeing Jesus in Each Other ... 9
5 The Importance of How We Were Birthed ... 11
6 Christ Is the Lifestyle of the Church ... 17
7 The Church: An Open Fellowship ... 21
8 A Church That Will Be a Feast of Freedom ... 27
9 Life out of Death ... 33
10 The Key: Who Are You, the Believer? ... 35
11 Acceptance and Accepting ... 37
12 The Church Will Be a Church of the People ... 41
13 The Church as a Family, Birthed by the Father ... 45
14 Spontaneous Ministers ... 49
15 A Family Operation ... 51

## Part II - Watchman Nee

16 The Basis of Unity ... 57
17 Seven Factors in Spiritual Unity ... 61
18 Seven Factors that Are Not Ground for Division ... 67
19 What Do You Do if You Are Displeased with the Church? ... 81

## Part III - Gene Edwards

20 Facing Some Harsh Realities ... 87
21 The Birth of a Curse ... 89
22 The Fathers ... 93
23 The Reformation and Curse Number Two ... 97
24 The Theological God ... 105
25 Do Ordinary Christians Want Division? ... 109
26 Step One: Becoming Honest About Unity ... 115
27 Step Two: A New Breed of Workers ... 121
28 The Christian Worker, Money, and Unity ... 125
29 The End of a Movement Mentality ... 127
30 Are You Ready for Unity? ... 133
31 Unity...Getting There ... 139

# Part I

## Warren Litzman

# 1

# The Shape of the Future Church

The church today is in a transitional state. Many watching this transition see a new day emerging for the church. They look upon the present church as it is and see its day coming to an end. Today's church has been a church that has tried to be a mighty army while at the same time being a stone edifice.

In my judgment, those who expect to see the church go on as it is are not in touch with reality. If we can take the pulse of God's people and sense the throb of their hearts, then we know that *this hour demands a radical rethinking* of the concepts and practices of the church of Jesus Christ.

It goes without saying that we will see no radical change in the universal body of Christ as a whole; nevertheless there *will be* change. It is coming. This change will take place on the local level, in a great ground swell among ordinary believers. It will be a repudiation of the church programs which have become slavery to the Lord's people rather than liberation and freedom in Christ.

## Four Factors

The church as it is expressing itself today has four distinct characteristics. They are doctrine, buildings, programs, and the clergy (pastors, preachers).

At first glance it would seem that a church could not operate unless it had these four elements. Yet not one of these is necessary for a body of believers to function, *nor* need they be necessarily *permanent* establishments for the expression of the body of Christ.

Movement away from these four predominant factors will take place as people who love the Lord and hunger for Him re-examine *going to church,...and* as they begin to know the liberation and freedom there is in Christ.

An informal gathering of believers is in contrast to so-called worship centers which have become places where preachers create a monument unto themselves by means of buildings. Buildings and preachers, in turn, are maintained by programs and doctrines.

After all, buildings, programs, etc. do not constitute the church.

It does not matter whether there are three thousand people meeting in a cathedral or three people meeting in a garage, Christ is no greater in one place than in another! The gathering together of the believers in Christ is a spiritual matter, just as worship unto God is carried out in spirit and truth.

Perhaps it is because it is the preponderance of these four elements—doctrine, buildings, programs and clergy—it seems to be innate to man's fallen nature to carry a secular attitude into the realm of things spiritual. For instance, look at Peter, James and John on the mount of transfiguration! They wanted to build a *building!* They wanted to erect a tabernacle to Moses, Elijah and Jesus. Believers today, like Peter, often find it hard to separate the *concept* of the church as a *building* from the *reality* of the church as the *body of Christ.* For them, going to a building is the same as going to *the church.* But the church being a building is a concept that did not come out of the Scripture. The church as a building is not something that will ever satisfy the hungry heart. Hungry hearts instinctively seek to be part of something that is an expression of no less than the Person of Christ. So also is the desire (and *need)* to *gather* as holy ones,... holy ones of like spirit and like understanding. This is an instinct innate to the Christian species.

To break out of the present mode will take daring: daring in thinking, in praying, in watching and in waiting. But out of this transition period which we are now in *will* come *hope*—hope for those who are hungry to know their God.

# 2
# Daring Is Needed for the Future Church

There is a growing number of spiritually hungry believers who sense that the church needs a radical change. That number increases with every passing day. What has brought on this grass-roots, almost worldwide, hunger? There are several contributing factors.

First of all, the church as it is expressed today is dominated by an over-clericalized *hierarchy* which does just about everything,...*especially* ministry. This practice cannot assuage the hungry heart. In the so-called megachurches of this era it is not unusual for fifty or a hundred ministers to be on staff. Such practice has produced a ministry and a program that is out of touch with the Lord's people; people who simply want to grow in the things of God with others.

Secondly, many churches have become *authoritarian.* Men who have reached great numbers of people begin to think that they are *more* important than *God* thinks they are! They are highly doctrinarian. Sometimes they are even ruthless in their dealings with God's people. Authoritarian ministers see sheep as only a means to an end—that is, a means to carry out their own *personal* ministry. Such men do not understand the nature of the church. It is sad that many of God's people who listen to these men do not sense what is happening to them. Unknowingly, they have lost their freedom in Christ.

Thirdly, today's churches are driven by *structure* and *statistics*. Churches have very earthly goals having to do with numbers and organization. Programs are approved only if they are found to be statistically sound in regards to (1) money and (2) the number of people involved or the number of people that might be reached by that particular program.

The criterion for success in churches today is *buildings*. How many buildings and the *size* of these buildings are what seem to matter... along with the *numbers of people* and the *amount of money* given. Spiritual success, unbelievably, is measured by how big your church is, how many you have reached, and how much money you take in. Added to that might be how *prosperous* the minister is.

The level of spirituality is actually being calculated with a secular measuring stick. That measuring stick is called *success*. Born-again believers are being caught up in this secular measurement instead of growing into the fullness of Christ. However, at the same time in which these numbers are growing, the number of people seeking a different kind of church and another way to worship God is *also* growing!

Why is the church the way it is, today? And why this worldwide hunger for something higher?

# 3
# A Loss of the Centrality of Christ

The ultimate reason the church is going to experience radical change is that today's church is missing its centrality—the centrality of Jesus Christ. We have lost sight of the Christ who not only died for us but *who now lives in us*.

Religion today has become an end within itself.

The passion to live by the life of Another has been lost. Yet those who walk in the Spirit, and those who *seek* to walk in the Spirit, are hungering to know their Lord. They will not long suffer the programs that deny them the fullness of Jesus Christ.

Change is inevitable. It *is* coming.

Right now believers are caught up in a "do-er" religion. Pause for a moment and look around. Christians are constantly *doing*, and *giving money*.

Doing has become the means by which people follow God.

This is a denial of the family relationship that we all inherit when we are birthed by God the Father. The absence of that family relationship in the life of a believer *must* cause Christians inevitably to become seekers of something higher than what they now have.

Unfortunately, many have been led to believe that giving money, building a new building, and carrying out their minister's program is actually entering into an intimate relationship of the Christ-life! Unbelievable!

This, of course, is not so.

There is a word that needs to be given to such seekers: If you are to share in Christ's suffering, pain, and conflict, you cannot isolate yourself from sharing in the lives of those who are oppressed.

The church today, either consciously or unconsciously, wants to spare us all from the kind of hurt that is akin to the hurt experienced by Christ who is in us. Anytime religion promises to spare us from pain and from death it is in fact taking away our very life as followers of Christ!

As surely as day follows night there will emerge a new, simpler, and Christ-centered expression of the body of Christ.

What will that expression of the church look like?

# 4

# The Importance of Seeing Jesus in Each Other

It is when believers see Christ in each other that a true bond of fellowship arises. That fact is one of the most important elements needed for unity in the body of Christ. The truth of "Christ in you and Christ in me" is the one ingredient so overwhelming that it dissolves the barriers between God's people.

Paul once faced Christians who were stepping back from one another, drawing lines between Jews and Gentiles. This is what he had to say to them.

> When you receive one another, you do as Christ did when He received *you.*
> (Rom 15:7)

There are multitudes of Christians right now who are disenfranchised and lonely because of man-made issues which have risen to divide them from others and separate them from fellowship that is innate to us all. God allows this loneliness in the lives of believers. Why? In order to push the lonely to Christ. The Lord will not take away this loneliness in believers until their hungry hearts see Christ in one another. This tears down the walls that separate them from becoming one. That is the only cure for the loneliness of believers.

Right now believers have a real problem accepting one

another. They don't recognize the fact that Christ is in every believer. Nor have they seen that Christ dwelling in us makes us *one* in Him.

If history has taught us anything, it is that preaching (no matter how insightful or moving it may be) will never take the place of the believer's instinctive hunger for fellowship with all other believers.

# 5
# The Importance of How We Were Birthed

Every believer in the body of Christ has been birthed by one element which is common to us all. That element is God the Father. We are all kin! You and I, and *all* of us who are believers, are kin. Whenever believers gather together, no matter where they meet, they are biologically kin and they *are* the body of Christ. Not only are we kin, not only are we one body, but we are also a family. *One* family. When believers begin to view one another as family members they will be able to wholly accept one another *apart from all other influences!* The instinct to do so is inborn to those who are kin.

Now look at this picture. A large group of lonely people gather together in a big building. They sit. Unmoving, they sit and listen to ministry from *one* person. Eventually that one person's doctrine becomes law to them. *Doctrine* is what they have in common with one another. *Not* an indwelling Lord, but a *doctrine*. On top of that, it is doctrine that is *disputed.* This minister is actually speaking against the teachings of another preacher (in another large building just down the street, who is also speaking to lonely people who are allowed *only* to sit and listen) and is disagreeing violently with the doctrinal view of that other minister.

Why is doctrine so powerful? Doctrine has an element of *security* in it *and* an element of *bonding*. Doctrine is what causes those people to come back again and again to the same building, the same program, and to *that* speaker. However, there is no real family spirit among God's people who do this. Acceptance flows from the ministry rather than from a Lord who is in each one of them.

One day this *will* change, and Christ will be our center.

### A Text to Live By

As we walk in the Christ-life, let's hold as our banner these words:

> "Wherefore from now on we know no man after the flesh. Though we have known Christ after the flesh, from now on we will know him that way no more." (2 Cor. 5:16)

When Christ becomes known as the life of believers, His life (the Christ-life) becomes all that believers *see* and all that believers *know* about one another!

We are in the body of Christ as a living experience. We no longer know another believer outside of his relationship to Christ. We accept the other believer as a person who is also related to Christ. We do not accept other believers by what they *do,* nor do we accept them on the basis of *how* they express Christ, nor by what their doctrine is. We accept other believers on the grounds of the Christ who is in them!

We accept other believers because they have been birthed by the *same* Father and they have the *same* Lord in them. You see, God has but *one* Seed and that one Seed is *Christ!*

Unfortunately, today's church has a substitute for Christ. *Doctrine* has become the grounds for Christians accepting one another.

Christians in today's churches (and those of past centuries) have accepted—or rejected—one another on the basis of doctrinal *beliefs*. Only on the basis of doctrinal belief. There is no scriptural ground for such a practice. Think of the implications! If you and I have differing views, we cannot accept one another! Christ accepts both of us, but we refuse to accept each other.

Acceptance is reserved solely for those who have similar beliefs. (The more exacting the doctrinal agreement the more acceptance.) As a result, we end up excluding members of our own family! We reject our very own kin.

It is my judgment that unless we shed such narrow-mindedness and catch a glimpse of God's great plan, we will *never* be totally secure in our walk with the Lord.

This practice of making doctrine a test of fellowship *must end.*

Never forget that it was Christ who, by His passion on the cross, made each one of us acceptable to God. If you are acceptable to God, what possible reason could I find to make you unacceptable to me! You should accept me because God has accepted me. I *do* accept you. Why? Because God *has* accepted you. When we believers recognize this simple fact of acceptance, we are immediately freed from *self-confirmation!*

As we see His acceptance of us, we become open to one another, *and* to all other believers. Prejudices fall away just as scales fall from our eyes. We see one another in a totally different way. In that wonderful moment, we see that different beliefs are not nearly as important as loving one another.

*Kinship is more important than doctrine!* Never reject your kin over doctrine.

## Knowing One Another in Spirit

I mentioned 2 Cor. 5:16. The second part of that verse contains the most radical theme I have found in Scripture.

It says that we are not even to know *Christ* after the flesh! What a powerful statement.

This verse refers to that time when Christ, incarnated, lived among men in bodily form in Nazareth, Galilee, Samaria, and Judea during the three years of His ministry. That was when He was God come in the *flesh*. Are we not to know this Jesus? Well, remember, your Lord is not in Galilee today; He left this earth. He *did* ascend! He reigns in the heavenlies. And He now indwells you! *This* is the Lord we are to know now! And this is the glorious One who lives in you.

Here is the point. None of us can live exactly like the Lord did when He lived on earth. We can express the Lord only as He presently lives in us and lives out through us. He operates through us, showing that part of Himself that is unique in you, and that which is unique in me.

Every believer has the same Lord in him. Unfortunately, not every believer will understand this fact or come to accept it. We must come to *know* that He lives within us...as our very life. That fact is not well-known, so many believers will be unable to express the Lord who is in them. (Nonetheless, there are *no* second-class citizens.)

To make Christ known is the work of the Holy Spirit. The ministry and work of the Holy Spirit is to cause the believer to begin to walk according to the Christ who is in him. The Christian who discovers an indwelling Lord, by means of the work of the Holy Spirit in Him, will always see doctrinal division fading away.

When believers gather (knowing Christ is in them and knowing He is their very life), they will express the Lord. Each will express Him in proportion to his level of understanding. You and I must accept any and every believer into our gathering regardless of the depth of that believer's understanding. Why? Because Christ is in each one. Full fellowship will be manifest only as believers see the plan of God and discover one another in Christ. These believers will gravitate together.

This means that, as we gather, we accept one another's differences and we downplay conflicts and criticisms. We do this simply because we have found the joy of fellowshiping with each other.

We are kin to one another. We are genetically bound by one common life. Remember, we all have but one Father in common. Although our growth in the Lord and our understanding of what He is doing in us may create various expressions in the body of Christ, we should never allow our understanding of Scripture or doctrine to cause division. (Or even the fact that *some* of us see that we are members of a family while others do not!)

The church of Jesus Christ is first and foremost a family that has been birthed by one Father. We are no longer just individuals. *We are a family in which everyone accepts the other in the same way they were accepted by Christ.*

This family spirit is greatly lacking in the present church, but it will be at the center of the ecclesia in the years to come.

Most believers have great difficulty even shaking hands with one another when they meet at a Sunday morning service. Certainly most never get a hug! In a fellowship where Christ is the life of each believer, people openly recognize each other as family members and greet each other just as family members do. As members of a family we Christians *should* greet each other with a hug. We are keen to make each believer feel that he is as loved by the Father as anyone else is. We bring this fact into reality by our actions. How? By our *acceptance* of each believer, and by our *actions* toward him. Consider, then, the way you overtly communicate to another believer that you accept him.

This family which you and I belong to is a *very* big family. The family we are talking about is not the sum of those who happen to be members of any one specific church. Rather, this family is the sum of all those who have been birthed by God the Father, *everywhere*. Such acceptance is not extended only to believers who are just in your locale, but wherever believers meet *anywhere* on earth.

Family life within the body of Christ affirms that no one is alone, no one has to bear his problems alone, and no one has to conceal his disabilities or his inabilities. Nor are there just *certain* ones who have a say in the body of Christ as over against others who have *no* say at all. No one is ignored or isolated because of his age or status.

Let each one *bear* the other, *forebear* the other, and put up with one another, even when it is unpleasant—yes, and even when there is *no* agreement!

Though family living of this nature is virtually unknown to most churches, it *is* the future.

# 6
# Christ Is the Lifestyle of the Church

There is a lifestyle reflected in all Christian gatherings. The lifestyle of a gathered body of believers is the Christ-life. That lifestyle is characterized and shaped by the very gospel of Christ!

Paul told the Philippians to let the manner of their lives be worthy of *the gospel of Christ.* Paul was saying that the lifestyle of believers should be qualified by the Lord who is in them.

Exactly what is "the gospel of *Christ*"*?* What is this glorious gospel of Christ that causes us to have a certain lifestyle when we meet? *His* gospel is the gospel of *freedom.* He has called us into a freedom we have never known or experienced before . . . anywhere! The expression of this freedom is a large part of the expression of the church.

Christ has given us the means and the freedom to experience the living God. Understand this about freedom: Freedom is evangelical, *not* legalistic. Freedom in Christ comes about in a believer's life by the gospel of Christ. There is a decisive difference between being free to experience the birthing of Christ within us as over against the legalism under which so many believers live.

Legalism means law; legalism means adherence to

man-made ideas. All those rules, programs, doctrines, and ideals you find in so many gatherings are there in order to keep a man-made program going! And—note this—when you are under such law, you also express a certain lifestyle. But it is a lifestyle expressed quite differently from the one when you gather in the freedom of Christ! The lifestyle of law is expressed very differently because it is determined by rules, prohibitions, restraints, regulations, peer pressure *and* an invisible (almost imperceptible) atmosphere of *conformity*. Life under the law is a formal, repressed, and agonizing expression.

Many churches today have a law that demands *uniformity*. Simply put, this means everyone must do (or abstain from doing) certain things. And you must do those things in exactly the way demanded!

Any time a born-again believer's lifestyle is expressed through legalism, the Lord who is within that believer *is of no avail to him!*

If you are in a place where every one must adhere to a rule, law, or program, then know that you are in a place that is *man-made*. Law in the church can continue to exist only if *man* is there to enforce the law!

The Christ who dwells in you is free to operate through you. Consequently, the lifestyle of the church is *free-flowing*. At the same time, the Holy Spirit's mission is to reveal Christ in you. In Christ and through the Holy Spirit there is no need for enforcement of law. Once a believer sees that Jesus Christ is his very life, that believer will adhere to all the commands that come out of the *cross!* That believer will instinctively adhere because he will have an overwhelming need to do the will of the Father. And...he will do the will of the Father, not by human effort but by the means of the life of Christ in him.

There will come a day when the church is made up of people who express a lifestyle that is not bound by a list of do's and don'ts. They will not have to *do* something in order to *be* something. *Rather, by knowing who they are in Christ, such a people will spontaneously do all the things the divine nature within them demands.* They will not do so by their own effort, but by the very Life that lives within them.

When Jesus began his ministry, He was different from any other prophet the Jews had ever seen. He was not sanctimonious! He did not put on airs! He did not act spiritual or religious. He *knew* who He was. He walked in the knowledge that His Father dwelled in Him. When we know who we are in Christ (by the birthing of the Father's life within us) we begin to walk in that same life regardless of what others say, do, teach or demand! And when a group of people walk in His life and in His freedom, they reflect the very lifestyle of Jesus.

## A Lifestyle Of Joy and Happiness

If a Christian lives by the law, and if he fellowships with a church that preaches law, it would be difficult for that person to fellowship with believers who live by a Lord who is within them. However, the Lord is raising up believers who live by His life. These believers will be as a stream running through the world, flowing right out of the loins of Almighty God.

They will be a people free to be who they are.

They will be a people free from man's harassment and dictatorship. They will be a people who have discovered that Christ is their life. They will be a people who are free to live that life regardless of what others think or do.

This freedom will change homes, it will change marriage relationships, and it will change business dealings out there in the world.

If you are a believer, then know that Jesus Christ lives in you. You are free because Christ Himself operates in you. What joy and happiness can flow from the life of a believer! However, that is not to say that there isn't any suffering in your life as a believer. There *is* suffering.

*Nonetheless the expression of the ecclesia is one of joy.*

Look around you. Everywhere you look you can see that the fun has gone out of the Christian life! God has an intention. That intention is that He have pleasure in us; that we have joy and happiness in being with Him and in Him, and He in us. When a group of believers who have a revelation of an indwelling Lord get together, they express joy and happiness just in being together and being with their Lord together. There is joy despite the difficulties they encounter from time to time.

The church in this hour is living under laws, regulations and teachings, and has lost much of the fun of being the church. The church has lost the pleasure of knowing the Lord Jesus and the Father. However, with the discovery of the Christ-life there will grow up a lifestyle of the church that is one of happiness and joy.

# 7
# The Church: An Open Fellowship

The fellowship of the body of Christ must always be open to anybody and to everybody. The theme of believers who are functioning in a denomination-free atmosphere and a classless society is a theme of the revelation that Christ is in us.

Jesus Christ is our hope in glory. *That* fact has created our fellowship. When we see that Christ in us is the hope each of us has, not only for salvation but also for resurrection, how can we build barriers?

What of those who say you must have certain spiritual experience in order to be one with the rest of God's people? Such a view is not reflective of one who has experienced "Christ in us." There must be *no* dividing or separating points between believers. There is no basis for division based on spiritual experience *or* revelation... not to mention doctrines and visions.

All that is necessary for a person to be a full-fledged, bonafide offspring of God is simply to believe on the Lord Jesus Christ. If anything else is added (such as membership, water baptism, some kind of deeper experience, or even a probational period), then the birthing of Christ in him is nullified by the acts of *man*. No man has the right to nullify what God has done.

Look again at our earthly families. When a newborn

baby is born, he becomes a full member of his family, does he not?

Have you ever known anyone to look at a newborn baby and say, "Well, I wonder if you are going to steal? If you do steal, you cannot be a bonafide member of this family. If you don't get the same kind of education the rest of this family has, you will not be a full-fledged member of our family."

No one does this. You will always be a member of your biological family.

Most parents look upon their newborn and receive him with joy, do they not? You want to make him laugh, do you not? You want to make him happy. It should be the same way with new converts coming into a functioning body of believers.

A fellowship of believers in Christ should always be an *open* fellowship. There is nothing in the Christ-life to join. You already have a membership in the family of God by having been birthed there. There can be *no other* requirements for membership.

Most important, believers must never be stereotyped according to their level of understanding. No one should be treated differently because he lacks the experience or understanding of other members of the gathering.

One of the problems of present-day Christianity is that the ministry has ceased to preach the gospel and, instead, preaches a program. To illustrate: When a certain message is being promoted in the church, suddenly that theme seems to appear throughout all the Scripture! As a result, these men of God do not preach the gospel at all, but—rather—a program. Every time they go to the *Word* they find only that which reinforces their program. Consequently, God's people never hear a pure gospel.

A heavy burden of responsibility is placed upon those who minister, for it is their responsibility to minister *Christ*.

## Learning Christ

What is the real issue of life here on earth? Is it some business goal or some personal achievement? Is it to have a healthy body, to "live long and prosper," or to have the perfect marriage and/or the perfect family?

It is none of these superficial things.

The real issue of life is knowing the Lord who is inside you. If the gospel does not start and end here, the believers listening to the gospel *will* come under law. One day those believers *will be told,* in order to become one with others in that group, they *must* do this and they *must* join that and they *must* give such and such amount of money.

*That is law!*

Oh, that we might live in the simple truth that God wants to supply all our needs and answer all our questions by showing us more of His Son. *His* Son, the One who is in us! The church that will emerge from out of that gospel will not be made up of people who have completed a membership class.

No, the church is made up of believers who, by the very certificate of their spiritual rebirth, are *already* integral members in the body of Christ. Membership will not depend upon how many committees you have served on or on how much money you have given to the church. You will not be considered a member because of your boldness or because your personality traits have elevated you above others to leadership positions.

The church may always have leaders, but they will always reach their level of operation *by the Spirit,* and not by human abilities and efforts.

## Friendship

Those who have laid hold of Christ as their center will not maintain an *exclusive* circle of friendship within that body of believers. *Friendship* is not the unifying factor in the church.

Jesus was brought by His Father into this world that He might have fellowship with the oppressed. Your Lord spent His time in a corrupt society with despised humanity. If He had created a fellowship built on friendship with a select group, He would have had to *stay in heaven!*

Believers who live by the life that is in them cannot live that life in a closed circle made up of "the pious and faithful few." Or of friends! They can live out that life only in *open affection* and *public respect* for one another.

Through Jesus Christ, "friendship" has become an open term, including *all* believers.

The message of the revelation of Christ as our life belongs to the whole body of Christ, not just to some part that believes a certain way. Jesus Christ is the Alpha and the Omega. Therefore the Christ-life is the *first* message and the *last* message. Christ Himself will be the final message the Holy Spirit delivers to the church, just as surely as He was the first message of the Holy Spirit.

That message, the message of Christ, belongs to all believers. And, yes, to men and women out in the future who have yet to be saved. *All* have the right to hear the message of Christ in all its fullness. Therefore, you and I must never be part of anything which separates humanity from the hearing of the gospel, for the gospel is God's message to *all* men. And if the gospel is for all men then the *fellowship* of the redeemed (the church) is for *all* who are redeemed! All! Do you fellowship with only a select part of the redeemed, that segment which believes as you do?

The gospel of Christ is a message that allows a person to be saved. Saved by the life of another.

As believers make Christ their all, the ecclesia (and the people within that ecclesia) will burst forth with the desire to share the gospel that has changed their lives. And those believers will receive *all* who receive the Lord.

There will be no human system by which the gospel spreads... *not* as it works out in the church today. No, the ministry of the church will expand because the Christians who are in that functioning body of believers have a burning desire to minister Christ. They will be encouraged to do so by everyone else who is in the gathering.

## Simplicity

The pattern of meeting will be a pattern of simplicity. Whether believers meet in a barn or in a home, they will meet simply. They will spontaneously reach the hearts of yet others who are not now being reached.

Outreach will be done in love.

## Leaving

When someone in the church feels it is time for him to leave a fellowship, love will triumph on both sides. You and I must never feel that our ministry is being hindered or hurt when other believers depart and do what they feel God has led them to do.

There will be gatherings of God's people where a believer will not feel in bondage to stay in that gathering, if he feels led of God to leave. As he goes from that gathering, he will know there will be no tearing down, no hurt, no pain inflicted by others. Those leaving and those staying will hug one another and move on to whatever the Father has called each of them to do.

A people who are unsectarian, who are loving, who are caring, who are free of doctrine and standards... such a people *will* exist on this earth. And their only doctrine will be Christ.

The day will come when the churches will always maintain open fellowship. After all, if there is nothing to join, there is nothing to break away from. Let our fellowship be in the bonds of love just as Paul so often wrote in his letters.

# 8
# A Church That Will Be A Feast of Freedom

If I use the word *fun* in this chapter to describe what I mean, I realize that it will immediately strike some readers as non-spiritual. (Perhaps that is why I use the term!) The majority of non-believers and churchgoers would tell you that the Christian life isn't supposed to be *fun*. It's not supposed to be out-and-out *fun* to go to a place where Christians gather to worship their Lord.

Yet for the believer, even the most serious matters in life ought to be faced *lightly*, because we have Christ in us. Read the New Testament from this view. Note that Paul seemed to take even the issue of death lightly.

> "Whether we live or die we are the Lord's!"
> (Romans 4:8)

This statement came from a man who found joy (and yes, I believe, even fun) in serving and living for his Lord.

I've noticed that believers often leave church services beaten and bowed down beneath a heavy load. These people are under such condemnation and guilt that to make it through life they have to literally play a game of fooling themselves.

Most Christian meetings are *law* meetings that put heavy emphasis on a Christian's *responsibilities*. "You, the Christian, can be blessed only if you give. If you want the Spirit of God, you have to tithe more."

The believer is also told over and over again how he should be using his time and what he should be doing with his life. In all this he is made to feel guilty if he does not live up to certain standards.

I wonder how many Christians have seriously considered never returning to Sunday morning church services... but return anyway because of *guilt?*

The same is true of giving, attending Sunday school, and other such things. "Present on account of guilt." Oddly enough, people stick with this kind of life. Dear, disillusioned, browbeaten hearts have no alternative, for that is the outcome of being driven by guilt. The fun of the Christian life has gone out of the Christian.

Gatherings of God's people are going to be marked by an atmosphere of freedom. Meetings will be a *feast* of *freedom.* A radical change is beginning to take place among God's people: Freedom is taking hold.

Whereas there is no external, visible Christ on earth today, no Jesus working in a carpenter's shop in Nazareth, today there is a Lord who is dwelling in His people. Jesus Christ is now birthed inside of us. God put the Lord Jesus in us as a gift. Our hearts crave for somebody to help us expand our knowledge of the Lord who is in us. He is there,... vibrantly alive. But God's people know so little about that glorious fact. Jesus Christ can move and work and live through us in ways we have never known. He does not give joy, He *is* joy. He does not give peace, He *is* peace. He does not give life, He *is* our life. We live by His life.

As the gospel is preached and as we learn such wonderful things about our Lord, we enter into a *feast*,... a feast unlike any we have ever known before.

Most of us started out in a religious atmosphere in which we were taught to fear God, not to enjoy him. We sat in church, and there—sitting—we were kept under control. We didn't dare do anything irregular. (That was true not only when we were children, but when we became adults as well.)

The very intent of the Sunday morning sermons, unfortunately, was to defend orthodoxy against heretics! Then there were also those sermons that demanded that we become more and more responsible. Whatever else it was, the Sunday morning worship service was certainly not designed for our enjoyment. We got the message, loud and clear! (Perhaps unconscious... but still very clear.) The message: *God doesn't allow any fun* when we are with Him in Sunday morning church services.

However, a dramatic change is under way. Meetings where Christ is our life will begin to embrace joy... *and* they will be *fun* meetings. If believers who gather together see only Jesus in one another and do not concern themselves with the grievous things others have done which fell short of certain standards,... *then* there is a *feast* of *life* in that gathering!

As we come together in our meetings without restrictions (and even with the freedom to move around during the meeting), while respecting the Word and respecting one another,... and with freedom enough not to stereotype anyone or anything according to some religious idealism,... *then* we will discover the enjoyment of *a feast of freedom.*

**The Ecclesia is a Celebration of Resurrection**

This feast, this gathering, is a festival of Christ's resurrection. He is alive! Not just alive, but alive in you, and alive in me. We, in turn, are alive now, and we are alive forevermore. We will never die in our spirits. We live now and on throughout eternity. You and I do not have to wait until our temporary body is replaced with a permanent one!

*Now,* through Christ in us, we can enjoy a freedom we

have never known before. We are free to worship God by our own unique expression. No one will ever say in such a meeting, "You are not what you ought to be if you do not come to the meeting," or…"because you do not give this much money," or…"because you do not live like the rest of us."

Those who have discovered that the Lord lives within them can never put the law upon another person or upon a people.

## Men Set Free

Men and women who have discovered that Jesus Christ is their all are a people who will have time to work Christ out in their lives without being put under pressure—the pressure of stereotyping typical of human organizations, or of a program pressed down on them.

Church life will not be enveloped with the erecting of buildings. It will not be a church with a program whose underlying purpose is to keep people under guilt. Rather, it will be a church where the ministry will be as free as the believers. It will be a gathering of people who allow Christ to work out of them. It will be a church where the only doctrine is Christ, and every other idea that does not begin and end with Christ will be of no effect. *Anything less than Christ will have little consequence among them.*

## Worship

Most importantly, this gathering of God's people, this feast of freedom, must have worship.

It is no wonder that the Scripture shows Christ attending a marriage feast! After all, gatherings are meant to be a celebration of Christ's resurrection life in us.

The Christ who is in you has been *married* to you. Therefore, there is oneness and union between the believers and the Bridegroom. It is *this* unity which makes it possible to gather in freedom. The Lord's earthly life was a festive, liberating and redeeming life. This same Lord—Jesus Christ—is in us. His resurrection from the dead is *the beginning of joy.* It is a joy that does not pass away, and ours is a celebration that will *never* end. Not on this earth, and not in the heavens.

Long ago, a gentleman named Hippolytus said, "The church is the bride who dances with Christ."

This spirit of joy will take hold of our meetings and exemplify our worship. Tears of sorrow, laments because we were not cared for, feelings of not being wanted, knowing we did not fit in, will be replaced with *laughter.*

The dead shroud of religion is swallowed up in victory. Cry out with Paul, "Oh death where is thy sting, oh grave where is thy victory?"

It has been far too long that meetings of worship to God have been bound by having to do things. Whether it was to sing a certain way or to pray a certain way or to live a certain way, it was *still* bondage.

And more death was worked into us than life.

As you behold a meeting of the body of Christ, look upon that worship gathering in a corporate sense. See that gathering for what it is. It is a gathering of family! When a family gathers, the members of the family are going to talk of things that are important to them. They are going to deal with issues that are important to *that* particular family. They are going to enjoy other members of the family because they are all kin to one another. After all, they *all* have a common father. What we wish to see in the Christ-life is a recapturing of the festive mood of the resurrection.

It will be a church that meets in the festivity of freedom,... a freedom that will be worked out right here on this earth to the glory of God.

The feast of freedom will be the hallmark of the gatherings. *Let the feast of freedom begin.*

# 9
# Life Out of Death

As we look at what the church will be in the coming years, I cannot help but reflect on the words of Jesus Christ,

> "Except a corn of wheat fall into the ground and die, it abides alone, but if it dies, it brings forth much fruit." (John 12:24)

I consider this one of the most important verses a believer can embrace. It is here that the Lord Jesus opens to you His relationship with the Father. But He goes even further to show us something about *who* the Father is.

The one thing our Father is, above all else: *He is a God with whom death is an essential to life.* This is what the church of Jesus Christ must understand. *Death* is an essential part of the Life of God.

The death aspect of God is woven into the very nature of God: *All life will come out of death.*

The message of the world, and our enemy, is the opposite: "Do this and this and you will have life...do this and this and you will be better off than you are now."

That was not the message of Jesus Christ. His message?

It is only as you become *nothing* that you can possibly ever be anything. And we will see the church embrace this truth to its very limits.

It is on the cross that God exemplified the true nature of His life. It was on the cross of Jesus Christ that we see the immovable principal that life comes only out of death. This is spiritual criteria. The present-day church is quick to get away from the message of the cross in the life of the believer. In fact, *the church of today will move away from this truth faster than any other truth.*

Yes, the cross is referred to in messages, but its practice, as seen in the very nature of God himself, is virtually unknown.

# 10
# The Key: Who Are You, the Believer?

The church will lay hold of the understanding of *life out of death* at the same time it lays hold of a deeper understanding of the Lord Jesus and a deeper understanding of the Father. Wrapped up in this understanding is also the unveiling of *who the believer is!*

If it is the nature of the God-life to blossom forth only out of dying, then you and I, who are partakers of the divine nature, will have this same reality as the force of our lives.

There is a unity among Christians who see Christ as life and see death as that which provides life. These believers instinctively know that they cannot find unity by theological strategy or ecclesiastical tactics. Oneness among believers can come only as they are drawn to the message of the cross! In response to that message, you *will* to stand under the cross *as your way of life.* The message of the cross tells all believers that life out of death is the path for all believers. The cross itself declares that this is the way of life for the church.

### Church

Jesus stated that life out of death would be part of the very essence of *communion.*

Your Lord wanted to be remembered for His shed blood and His broken body. Communion is a reminder of the nature of the God that is in you. Communion presents to you the message that *life comes only out of death!*

Leaving out this part of the gospel has brought about the hierarchy and the authoritativeness so often found in religion today. But when believers see what they have become in Christ, when they see the exalted place they have been lifted to by the death of Another, they also see that *they are acceptable to God.* Once a Christian sees this he looks around and sees that everyone else who is a believer is just as acceptable as he is!

Such a believer understands that it is only by the life of Another that we exist at all.

When you *ignore* life out of death, you begin to feel that you are something important within your own self. When you touch life out of death, you *know* that you are nothing. You also *know* that He is everything.

At the communion table the believer sees that when his old ways are broken, that breaking also works death in him *so that others might live.* Only in the death of Christ can you see the self-surrender of Christ to His Father. As we see Christ, self-surrendered to the Father, we surrender ourselves to Him also. This sight must transfix all believers who dare to gather as a body.

You will surrender to your Lord automatically as you see Christ as your very life. You will also see that you, and all other believers, are acceptable to the Father. There is a death that works in God. From out of this death and out of the life that comes from death, Christ's life is extended toward all believers.

# 11
# Acceptance and Accepting

One day we, as local bodies of believers, will refuse no believer. We will accept *every* Christian, knowing that he has the right to fellowship in the fullness of godliness. Neither you nor I can refuse anyone for this single reason: Christ's death and our death in Him has brought life to every one of us. I have no life of my own, nor do you. I have no life that is better than anyone else. You and I died in Christ; consequently, we are correct to accept anyone else who is in Christ. And we are not correct in excluding or holding back others from growing up in Christ. Your Lord will invite to His table *all* who are hungry and in need.

You and I step back from others' lives, letting others in the church have the freedom to live out who they are in Christ. This is not an act of graciousness, rather it is simply accepting that which is reality.

Consider this: Everyone of us has been justified by *someone* else. We are not justified by rules, and certainly you and I are not justified before God by anything we have ever done!

### Pain in Loss

There is pain to be experienced in church life. For instance, whoever embraces the cross of Jesus Christ in a serious way will feel pain when there is division in the body of Christ. (1 Cor.1:13.)

A fellowship of believers in which Christ is all, in which men and women are living Christ as life, will *almost certainly* share a great deal of *tribulation* and *persecution.* But this suffering only enhances fellowship with one another and with our Lord.

This is the testimony of people in our generation and many generations before:

> *"When I came into this understanding and when I came into fellowship with others who had seen Jesus Christ as their all, I suffered more than I ever had before."*

Why is this? It is because of your *identification* with Christ. It is because the God-nature in you works life *out of death.*

Expect such trials *even* if you live in a country *where there is freedom of religion.* Even in America, expect the church to suffer together as a committed people. Yes, there *is* fun and there *will be* fun; there is joy and there will be happiness in this new relationship with the Lord as you meet in the church. But there will also be hurt and suffering as you have never known before.

Do not be deceived to believe otherwise. Even Christians in the western world will not escape times of tribulation and pain. Such things seem to *always* come upon a body of believers who are being hammered together by the Holy Spirit. But remember that your anchor is in the cross.

*Your life comes out of Calvary.*

The church will be a church that accepts what God is doing in one another's lives. It is your belief in the Lord Jesus Christ that saves you. Believe on His finished work; do not believe on your works of righteousness to save you.

The church will be made up of believers who carry the cross. They will not carry it as a weapon or as a sign. They will carry the cross in such a way that they show forth their need of God.

# 12

# The Church Will Be A Church of the People

As we consider the future, I would like to call your attention to two kinds of churches which exist among us today.

These particular churches provide their people with their sense of identity and their sense of purpose. But at the same time, these churches introduce to the hearts of God's people ideas which work in conflict with one another.

The *first* of these two churches is the *hierarchical* church. Such churches are managed by "shepherds."

In these churches, you will hear such words as shepherding, authority, kingdom living, dominion, reconstruction, covenant people, God's government, etc. This type of church is really a stumbling block to the development of body life among believers. In this kind of church the clergy have great power. Christians in these groups are likened to a flock of sheep. They have nothing to say. They are oppressed by ecclesiastical overlords. You can almost compare the oppression in these churches with the world's political oppression. The people have to live with that power and they must either like it or be excluded.

The *second* kind of church, which is also a stumbling block to believers experiencing church life, is the one that demands everyone to live alike.

This is a *stereotyped* church, and God's people in it become stereotypes. If, as a believer, you become part of this kind of exclusive society, you will be among those who exclude all others. *You* are the *elite!* If you do not have membership in this group, if you do not believe what they teach about baptism, about the Spirit, about faith and whatever else they teach, you simply cannot be one of them. These are *not* churches of the people; these are *elitist* churches.

Both of these types of churches have something in common. The people who are enlisted therein are to be *conquered*. The *program* is primarily that of *conquering* God's people...conquering them in order that they all become alike. Their message says, essentially, "We must win other people to our doctrine; only among us are the people of God."

Such leaders may also claim that the gospel they preach is more beneficial...it is a better gospel than what is preached by others. Whatever they are saying, it comes down to this, "If you want anything positive in your life you must have our message." These churches have programs that are *for* the people, but the church is not *of* the people. The people are objects.

When believers lay aside such foolish concepts, the church will be a family. They will live by the life of Christ and they will recognize Christ in one another. They will be able to demonstrate Christ to all with whom they come in contact. Whether the believers are meeting together or eating a meal together, they express practical, concrete needs and consider practical solutions.

We must hear the gospel and then allow that gospel to work out of us. It is only when God's people have the gospel and are experiencing Christ that true church life works.

In the church of today, the preacher is the center. (Not

Christ, not the church, but the *preacher!)*

If the minister says, "God has told me to do this and this and I must be faithful to God and you must help me to be faithful to God," then God's people are *not* the center of that fellowship of believers. Christ and His people, not ministers, are supposed to be the center of the church. It is only when the message proclaimed maintains Christ as the all and in all that there will be life in that church, and the true *reality* of the church will come forth.

## Ministry or Church

If Christ and His people are the center, this places the ministry in a different light. As long as God's people wish to support the programs of a ministry, then that ministry should continue, but no longer than that! When people cease to want to carry out the program of the one ministering, then that ministry should *move on.* Ministry is subject to the church, not vice versa.

This principal will one day not only be practiced in the church, but will be advocated by both those being ministered to *and* the one ministering!

As to outreach, if the revelation of Christ is unfolded and if God's people experience the completeness of Christ, then they will attract other people to the ecclesia. At the same time, they will also be proclaiming the gospel of Jesus Christ. The message belongs to the people and the message is that Christ is all. We must understand that the believers who gather are members of the body of *Christ.* God's people belong to the *Father,* for *He* is the one who has birthed them.

Ministry, therefore, must ultimately be from the people and of the people.

All ministry should adhere to family needs. When family needs are not met, it is the *ministry* that is lacking. There is need of ministry, and that ministry makes the difference in the lives of God's people. It is true that no two people will ever be the same; therefore, ministry will express itself in several different ways. We see that God has created us differently, but we are all maintained by the same life. That life is Jesus Christ. We manifest the same God-nature which is in each of us.

Our cry to those who hinder the word of God is: Be faithful to the preaching of the gospel! The only thing which can make a difference in the life of the Lord's people is the proclamation of that one gospel which has *Christ* as our all. The *Logos* coming into the believer bears witness with the wisdom of Christ who is in that believer.

Something happens to each of us from *within* and *without.*

# 13
# The Church as a Family, Birthed by the Father

We would all agree that the church will never be what it ought to be without the Holy Spirit. But what is it that the Holy Spirit brings to the church? He shows us what we, as believers, *are*. . . in Christ. The Christ-life will be what forms the ecclesia; and it is the Holy Spirit who will cause this people—who share the life of God—to become a community of believers. The Holy Spirit will show each believer that the life he now lives is Christ. Each believer will know, by the work of the Holy Spirit, that he has a life in him that is not his own. It is the life of Christ!

You are birthed by God through Christ; and Christ, through you, will manifest Himself. The person that you are will be overwhelmed by the life of Christ within you. Your Lord gives life to you and overrides whatever part of you used to be the lead personality of your life; in that place Christ's own life is manifested in you.

You and I are a branch bearing the life of the vine. You and I produce the *fruit* that is of that vine. Christ is the vine and His life flows through the vine; in so doing He becomes the life and the personality of the branch. When the Lord Jesus Christ is so revealed in the believer, the believer will begin to manifest his Lord. A group of believers will do the same.

The church, in the eyes of God, is not made up of human egos that are doing as they please. In a true expression of the ecclesia you will find a church made up of members who express the Lord. Within that fellowship the gospel will be ministered, the gospel proclaimed; and the gospel will declare that the branch can do nothing without the vine. Christ will be manifested. He will manifest Himself and He will be that which is manifested.

On the cross man was given up for dead, and out of that death the believer exhibits a whole new life... Christ!

*"I no longer live, but Christ lives in me."*

This is Paul's witness. This will be the witness of every believer in the church. If I no longer live, if I am crucified with Christ, then I no longer have a ministry of my own. All ministry that flows out of me is Christ.

## A New Understanding of the Ministry

The future holds for us an emerging expression of the church that is simply a manifestation of Christ's own *ministries*. It will be *Christ-life* and ministries coming from the believer.

You have heard of the term, "the gifts of the Spirit," as mentioned in 1 Cor. 12. It would be far better if they were called "ministries of Christ." These are not *men's* gifts. Whatever it is that the Holy Spirit puts within a man is certainly *not* men's gifts. Those gifts are of the Lord, from the Lord, and by the Lord. If gifts come out of a man's soul, then they are soulish gifts. *Those* are simply talents of a man.

But if the gifts proceed out of the Holy Spirit? If this is the case, then always remember that the Holy Spirit's function, operation, and pleasure is to reveal *nothing* except the Lord Jesus Christ. In other words, the Holy Spirit simply reveals the *ministries of Christ*. These ministries can operate through every believer, within the church, by means of the administration of the Holy Spirit.

It should be pointed out that these are neither gifts nor ministries *for* individuals. All gifts—or ministries—are *for* the corporate body of Christ. When an organization speaks of Christians having gifts, and when they say to Christians, "You should use these gifts," they are outside the bounds of Scripture. The operations of the Holy Spirit and the ministries of Christ are *for* the church, *within* the church!

There are five ministries mentioned in Ephesians 4. These are not offices of men. Why? Because men are no longer to live as independent cells. Each of us is now alive only by Christ. What is done through us comes out of, and is done by, an indwelling Lord. Once again, all five of these ministries, or offices, are for the church and within the church.

All of them are Christ's offices! All are but expressions of Christ. These expressions of Christ come through the administration of the Holy Spirit, and it is *always* the *Lord* Himself who is expressed. Furthermore, the ministries of Christ can operate through any member of the body. When the Holy Spirit chooses to do so, He can designate *any* vessel for use. The weakest member of the body of Christ (and perhaps even the least honorable) has Christ within him. We cannot say what ministry will or will not come out of this believer.

It has been a long time now that men have been assuming positions for themselves. But men assume these positions outside the operation of the Lord who is within them. They also assume these positions outside the local body of believers. Such men see themselves as men raised up by God, but God only raises up Christ. As Christ becomes the life of a believer experientially, any and all believers share in ministry!

Ministry in the church will have one great distinction: Ministry will be Christ!

# 14
# Spontaneous Ministers

A great deal of emphasis is being put on *gifts* at this time, especially by para-church organizations. "What is your gift," is an often-asked question. However, it is not necessary for a believer to know how he is being used by the Holy Spirit! It is simply a matter of the believer arising in the morning and living that whole day being who he is in Christ. The Holy Spirit is able to work through the believer according to the will of God.

Did the Lord Jesus ever get up in the morning and try to be the Son of God? No. He simply *was* the Son of God.

Paul did not get up in the morning and try to live the Christ-life. He did not have to try because he had been birthed into this realm. Once a believer lays hold of this revelation, he is no longer attracted to the message that he must try to be that which he already is! The believer will simply and spontaneously live out his life, without such thoughts.

I have never once tried to be my mother's child; I simply am my mother's child. It never entered my mind that I was anything else. This is the gospel that needs to be proclaimed. All born-again believers are to know that they are who they are. You need not try to be a Christian; you *are* a Christian. You don't have to try to be a worker for the Lord; this is simply part of your everyday life!

Jesus Christ did not try to be Savior of the world. You do not need to try to be witnesses unto this world; *that is what we are.*

You may be a doctor, you may be a salesman, you may be a teacher. You do not try to be these things. In the same way, you and I are witnesses. First and foremost we are witnesses because that's who we are by birthing. To witness is something that comes out of our daily lives through our profession and social contacts. It is Christ alive within you every moment of every day, at all times. I can be nothing of myself, I can do nothing of myself, nor can you. It is Christ who *does*... in you... and through you.

# 15
# A Family Operation

We shall see a church emerge that will win the lost to God in the way they were intended to be won. All ministries will be part of the family because witnessing is a natural function of the family. We shall enter into the priesthood of the believers in actuality, not in theory. All of us were created different, but there is not one believer who has more of the Lord inside of him than another. God created us different so that we might express Christ differently. Some preach, some sing, some play an instrument. Some of us go into medicine and some of us go into the world of labor, and yet all of us have been rebirthed by God and we all express the same Lord.

Today you and I stand in a time of transition. There is so much unhappiness and unrest among believers everywhere. *Christians are tired of going to church.* They find church irrelevant and boring. The Holy Spirit will lead God's people into a new and vibrant relationship with God—and with other believers—that is not dissimilar from the family. Every birthed member of God's family is called to tell others about this birthing! We are to proclaim the gospel. This proclamation is not just for the lone theologian or evangelist; every person who has been birthed by our Father and learns who he is in Christ grows to understand family relationships—he shares such insights, experiences and realities wherever he goes and whatever he does.

## Summation

I make the following observations and proposals: Worship is still too much centered on the clergy and is too much organized around a pastor. Right now worship is centered in an organized congregation. Nonetheless, worship meetings should take place in the lives of believers in a way very similar to family relationships.

We will see radical changes in worship and in all gatherings when (1) there is time for all believers to share; (2) all Christians in the family of God greet one another as family—when we hug, when we embrace, when there is genuine and informal fellowship between us, when gatherings are real "family happenings"; and (3) not only the ministry prays and speaks, but when the family prays and speaks... as one.

We must see our meetings as a feast for the Lord and for His family. I am not speaking of just one Sunday nor am I speaking of just church gatherings. Every time a few of us get together, let it be a festive occasion of spiritual growth. Let it be a time of fun in the Lord.

What about the question of joining... of becoming a member? This idea should be lost in family relationship. The very nature of our faith in the Lord Jesus Christ means that we are one. We are one in Christ by a spiritual birth. We are *not* members of one another by anything *outward*. We are not members of one another by anything special we believe! It is the birthing that makes us family members.

This family relationship can exist only when God's people see Christ in each other. The love of God is experienced mostly by those who see Christ in one another.

A multitude of believers are famished today. They are

restless, wanting to know the Lord,... wanting to know a *loving* Lord. They know they do *not* have such a relationship with their God; yet this is the very thing for which God's people are crying. They wait for the day when that relationship is unfolded to them.

A church that *fits* God's people must be a church of love... love one for the other. However, that love must not be based on what one *does* nor on what one *believes,* but simply on the fact of *who* he is in Christ. The love of God is most often experienced in small gatherings, not in large organizations or institutions. The large mega-churches and the huge organizations have relieved most believers of their independence and their responsibility. But in times of hurt and times of persecution (and in times when the heart grows so hungry) the true body of Christ emerges. Only in the body are those needs met.

The individual who "goes to church" and returns to his world as one powerless and one suffering from inner doubt... that one remains a pawn to other forces. Only in the gathering of the family does the believer become one who is ready for action; and only there does he find the capacity to resist all those things which stand against him in this world.

Hope in the midst of conflict is sustained only when we are part of one another, when we are members one of the other, trusting each other... in a family atmosphere. Hope is embodied in the body of Christ. This is especially true among believers who have an understanding of "Christ in me and Christ in you." Such believers are ready to withstand this world.

Let us press toward the coming day.

# Part II

Watchman Nee

# 16
# The Basis of Unity

The church is made up of a vast number of believers, yet they live in different parts of the world, so how could they possibly be *one?* There are differences in their ages, there are differences in their social positions, differences in their education and background. There are differences in outlooks, in temperament, in culture. What is the secret of the unity of the saints? How could all of these people, with so many thousands of differences, become one?

It is not as though they had a grand convention at which they agreed to be one. Christian unity is no human product. The origin of unity is purely divine. This mysterious unity is planted in the hearts of all believers, for this unity is nothing less than the unity of the Spirit. (Eph.4:3)

Exactly what does "the unity of the Spirit" mean? There is a Spirit that dwells in your heart. This Spirit dwells in the hearts of all believers, and yet this Spirit is one. Because He is one and because He dwells in each one of us, He makes all of us one. He Himself is one; He is in all of us; we are one even as He is one.

You and I and all the other believers who now live, or who have ever lived, may have countless differences, but we have one fundamental likeness. *The Spirit of God dwells in every one of us.* This is the secret of the oneness of believers. Our unity is inherent in all believers and therefore makes us one. This inherent unity makes it impossible for there to be division between believers.

The only possible division between believers is that of *geography*. Space and time are our only differences as far as oneness is concerned. (That the Spirit is in us is also our reason for separation from the world.)

Those who do not have this unity of one Spirit are not our brothers. Those who have this unity *are* our brothers, and there is no division. In other words, if you have the Spirit of Christ in you and I have the Spirit of Christ in me, then *we both belong to the same church.*

You and I are united! We are united by one Spirit and that Spirit dwells in both of us. Paul said to the believers in Ephesus, "Keep the unity of the Spirit." Notice that he did not exhort us to "get" this unity. He merely said to *keep* it. *We already have unity.* We need only *keep* the unity we have. God has never told us to become one with other believers! We *are* already one with other believers. We do not need to create unity, we need only to *maintain* the unity we already have.

Neither can you and I *break* this unity. We are one in Christ by the Holy Spirit. It is remarkable that you and I cannot break the unity. To break this unity would mean you would have to rid yourself of the Holy Spirit. Your unity with all other believers is an eternal fact—in Christ.

Unfortunately, there is something we can do. We can *destroy the effectiveness* of our unity with one another. When that happens, the expression of the church is lost. When the expression of unity is lost, we have not only failed to preserve this precious unity; we have also destroyed the *fruit* of our oneness. Today, therefore, there is little outward sign of this wonderful unity we all have as children of God.

Are we supposed to determine *who* our brothers and sisters are in the church of God?

We must not say to another one, "Do you hold the same doctrinal views as I do?" We must not ask, "Do you have the same spiritual experiences that I have?" You must not inquire as to another believer's customs, his mode of living, his interests or preferences, and then tally them up to see if they agree with ours.

There is only one inquiry which will tell.

"Are you indwelt by the Spirit of God?"

We cannot ever insist on a unity of *opinion*. We cannot insist on a unity of *experience*. We cannot insist on *any* unity among believers except the unity of the Holy Spirit who dwells within us and who has made Christ one in us. That is the unity which must always be among the children of God.

*All* who have this unity *are* in the church.

Surely you have had the experience of being on a train or a plane or a boat, meeting a stranger, talking with him, and, as your conversation ensued, finding that you had a pure love for this person welling up within your heart. This spontaneous love flowing out of you happens because there is one Spirit dwelling in both of you. Such inner, spiritual oneness transcends all social differences, all racial differences, and all national differences.

How can you know that this other person has this unity of the Spirit? Right after Paul said for us to keep the unity, he had something else to say. He pointed out what it was that believers had who possessed this unity. There are seven things which all believers naturally share. By the existence of these seven elements (or the lack of them) we can know whether or not a person has the unity of the Spirit. True, there are other things that may be very important, but here are seven things that are *vital*. In fact, these seven elements are *indispensable* to spiritual fellowship. These seven points are at once both the minimum *and* the maximum requirements that can be made of anyone who professes to be a believer. (You *can* expect a professing Christian to have these before you extend fellowship and acknowledge oneness in the church... but you can make *no other* demands!) We will look at these seven elements in the next chapter.

# 17
# Seven Factors in Spiritual Unity

> "There is one body and one Spirit, even as also you are called in one hope of your calling. One Lord, one faith, one baptism, one God who is the Father of all, who is over all, and through all, and in all."

You are a member of the church on the reference ground that you possess the unity of the Spirit. Possessing this unity of the Spirit results in your being one with all believers on all the following seven points. These seven elements are parts of that unity of the Spirit. These seven elements are the common heritage of *all* the Lord's people. You *can* draw a line of demarcation between those who belong to the church and those who do not, but it must be nothing beyond these seven points; otherwise, you will exclude someone who belongs to the family of God. We dare not require anything less than these seven elements; we dare not add anything more. Those people in whom all these seven elements are found belong to the church. All who lack them do *not* belong to the church.

### One Body

There is membership in the body of Christ. The sphere of our fellowship is the sphere of the body. Those who are outside the sphere of the body have no *spiritual* relationship with us. Those who are inside the sphere of the body are *all* in fellowship with us.

You cannot make any choice of who you will fellowship with in the body. You cannot accept *some* members and reject *others*. Everyone of us is a part of one body. Nothing can possibly separate us from the body of Christ; therefore, nothing can separate us from one another.

Any person who has received Jesus Christ belongs to the body of Christ. You... and I... *and* all other believers, are one, and we are all one with Christ.

If you and I do not wish to extend fellowship to a certain person, we must first make sure that he does not belong to the body of Christ. If he does belong to the body of Christ, we have absolutely no ground to reject him.*

### One Spirit

If someone comes seeking fellowship with you, he may be very different from you in experience or in outlook; but if he has the same Spirit dwelling in him which you have dwelling in you, he is entitled to be received as a brother. If he has received the Spirit of Christ and if you have received the Spirit of Christ, then you are one in the Lord. *Nothing* must divide you.

### One Hope

There is a common hope among all the children of God—not a general hope, but a *specific* hope. That hope is the hope of our calling. What is our hope, as Christians? We hope to be with the Lord in glory forever. There is not a single soul who is truly the Lord's in whose heart there is not this hope. To have Christ in you is to have the hope of glory in you. (Col.1:27) If anyone claims to be the Lord's but has no hope of glory, he has a mere empty

---

*Unless for some reason he is under discipline; and these things must be clearly laid down in the Word of God.

profession of what he claims to have faith in. All who share this one hope are all one.

*Since we have this hope of being together for all eternity, how dare we be divided in time!* We cannot be. We are going to share the same future; shall we not gladly share the same present?

## One Lord

There is only one Lord; He is the Lord Jesus Christ. All who recognize that our God has made Jesus of Nazareth to be both Lord and Christ... those very ones are one with you. They are one with me. And together, we are all one in Him. If anyone confesses Jesus to be Lord, then the Lord whom he has is also our Lord. And the Lord we have is His Lord. We serve the same Lord; therefore, nothing whatsoever can separate us.

## One Faith

The faith which Paul speaks of here is *the faith.* This is *not* speaking of our faith as regards doctrine. This faith has nothing to do with the interpretation of Scripture on points of doctrine. *This* faith is the faith through which we have been saved! This faith is the faith that is the common possession of all believers. This is the faith that Jesus Christ is the Son of God; this is faith that He died for the salvation of sinners; this is faith that He lives again to give life to the dead. Any person who lacks this vital faith does not belong to the Lord. On the other hand, all who possess this faith are the Lord's. The children of God may follow many different lines of scriptural interpretation, but in regard to the fundamental faith, we are one. Those who lack this faith have no part in the family of God. Those who have this faith are those whom we must recognize as our brothers and sisters.

## One Baptism

Does this baptism refer to baptism by immersion? Or

does it refer to baptism by sprinkling? And is this a single baptism, or a triune baptism?

There are various methods of baptizing accepted by God's people. If we make *the form* of baptism a dividing line between those who belong to the church and those who do not, we shall exclude many true believers from fellowshiping with us. There are believers who sincerely believe that a physical baptism is not necessary; nonetheless, they are children of God. We dare not, for that reason, exclude them from the fellowship.

What, then, does "one baptism" mean?

Paul throws light on this subject in his first letter to the Corinthians:

> "Is Christ divided? Was Paul crucified for you? Or were you baptized into the name of Paul?" (1 Cor.1:13)

The emphasis here is not on the *method* of baptism; the emphasis is on the *name* into which you are baptized. The first question is not whether you are sprinkled or immersed or dipped, or dipped three times or one time. The important point is: In whose name have you been baptized? If you were baptized into the name of the Lord, that is your qualification for church membership! If anyone is baptized into the name of the Lord, I welcome him as my brother. Regardless of the method of his baptism, I welcome him as my brother.

I do not imply here that it is of no consequence whether we are sprinkled or immersed, or whether or not our baptism is spiritual or literal. The Word of God teaches that baptism is literal and that it is by immersion. Nonetheless, the point Paul makes here is that the *method* of baptism is *not* the ground of our fellowship! The name into which we are baptized is the ground for fellowship. All who are baptized in the Lord Jesus Christ are one in Him.

### One God

Do we believe in the same personal, supernatural God? Do we believe Him to be our Father? If so, then we belong to the same family. We *are* one family. There is no adequate reason for our being divided.

* * *

These seven points are the seven factors in divine unity. That divine unity is the possession of all the members of the divine family. These seven factors constitute the only test of Christian profession! Every true Christian, no matter where he is, what age he lives in (or once lived in), no matter his customs, race or color, he possesses these elements. Like a seven-fold cord, the unity of the Spirit binds all the believers throughout the world.

No matter the diversity of character or circumstances, if we have these seven expressions *of inner oneness* then there is nothing that can possibly separate us from one another.

If you impose any condition of fellowship beyond these seven, then you are guilty of sectarianism. You are making a division between those who are manifestly the Lord's people. If you apply any test but these seven; if you test fellowship on ground of immersion, or some interpretation of prophecy, or some teaching regarding holiness, or a pentecostal experience, then you are imposing conditions other than those stipulated in the Word of God.

All who have these seven points in common with us are our brothers. Whatever their spiritual experience may be, or whatever their doctrinal views or church relationship may be, they are still our brothers.

Neither can you say to someone, "You must come out from all that contradicts our oneness." (We cannot make a requirement that anyone resign from any denomination.) Our oneness is based upon the actual *fact* of our oneness!

That oneness is made real in our experience by the indwelling Spirit of Christ!

* * *

These are the seven elements of unity. Now let us look at seven things that are *not* valid points of division.

# 18

# Seven Factors That Are Not Ground for Division

Most believers today are blind to the basis of what constitutes a church and what does not.

When someone asks a Christian, "To what church do you belong?" the first thought that enters that Christian's mind is that this question is about (1) the specific line of teaching he approves of, or (2) how his specific group is different from another group.

How few would answer the way a first-century believer would have answered, "I belong to the church in Ephesus," or "I belong to the church in Corinth," or "I belong to the church in Jerusalem," or "I belong to the church in Antioch." Who would answer today, "I belong to the church in London," or the church in Shanghai, or the church in New York or Orlando.

Note that, concerning separation from the world, you are separated because you are in Christ. It is our being in Christ that separates us from the world. But what of separation from other believers? That you live in one city and I live in another causes you and me to be separated from one another. Here is the only reason for separation: We live in different cities!

The only reason that you are separated from any other believer is that the two of you live in two different places.

The only reason that I do not belong to the same church as some other believer is because I do not live in the same city that he lives in. Now that is division caused simply by space... by geography. *There is no other division between us!*

Note that this is separation that is *positive!* If I wish to be part of the same church that you are part of, then obviously I must simply pack and move. I move to the place where you live. On the other hand, if you and I occupy the same space at the same time (that is, if your residence and my residence are in the same community) but I do not wish to be a member with you in the same church, then I have a problem and the only solution is for me to move to another city. There is *no* other ground given to Christians for division.

* * *

Let us look now at seven things over which we must never separate ourselves from other Christians.

We first looked at the positive side of unity among believers. We saw that these elements are ordained by God to make us one. Now let us look at things over which Christians should never divide and over which a church should never be divided.

## Spiritual Leaders

You are very familiar with the passage in 1 Corinthians that reads as follows:

> I am of Paul, I am of Apollos, I am of
> Cephas and I am of Christ. (1 Cor.1:24)

Paul tells the Corinthian believers they are carnal because they have been sectoring themselves off in the church in Corinth. By divine ordering, those believers in Corinth are indivisible. Nonetheless, the believers—though they were not actually involved in division—*were* showing *favoritism.* Favoring what? They were showing favoritism towards certain Christian *workers*. Some believers in Corinth said that they enjoyed Apollos' approach the most. (He appealed to the Greeks in the Corinthian church.) Other believers liked Peter best. (Peter appealed to the Jewish nature.) Then there were those who were boasting that they were of Paul, their founding apostle. Perhaps the most *subtle* divisiveness of all came from those who were claiming that they belonged only to Christ.

Here are Christians sectoring themselves off on the basis of the leader they liked the best.

### Division Along the Line of Liking or Disliking a Christian Worker

Peter was a zealous minister of the gospel. Paul was a man who had suffered much for his Lord's sake. Apollos was one whom God had certainly used in His service. Without question, all three men had been used of God in the church in Corinth. But God does not permit the church to make Christian workers the ground for division. Certainly there is no excuse for separating yourself from other believers because *you* do or do not agree with a Christian worker. The Lord did not ordain that His church be divided on the basis of *persons*.

It was all right to have a church in the city of Corinth. It was all right to have a separate and different church in Ephesus. It was quite all right to have several different churches in a province called Galatia (but only one church in each town in that province). It was all right to have different churches in different cities in a nation which was called Macedonia. It was all right for the believers to esteem their leaders whom God had used among them. But it would have been wrong for them to divide a church according to the leaders who had helped them.

Paul, Peter and Apollos were true-hearted servants of God. Those men had allowed no party spirit to separate between the three of them. It was their devotees—their self-proclaimed followers—who were responsible for this segmenting of the church in Corinth.

This is a tendency of human nature. We delight to show preferences for those who appeal to us the most. The source of this is our carnal nature. So many of God's children know little or nothing about the power of the cross to deal with the flesh, and this was such an instance.

This tendency to place an esteemed man above the unity of the church has expressed itself frequently throughout church history. Much damage has been wrought as a consequence.

It *is* in keeping with God's will that we should learn from spiritual men. It is in keeping with God's will that we profit by their leadership. But it is *contrary* to God's will that we should divide the church according to the men we admire or men we dislike. The Christian workers in this passage of Scripture would have none of this.

The only scriptural basis for the forming of a church is difference in space... in geography; that is, the difference in city limits between towns and cities, *not* on difference of leadership.

### Instruments of Salvation

If liking or disliking Christian workers is not ground for dividing the church, neither is there ground for dividing the body of Christ over the person who led you to Christ.

Some of the Corinthian believers proclaimed themselves to be of Peter, of Paul, or of Apollos. They traced the beginning of their spiritual history to one of these men; consequently, they thought they *belonged* to that man. It is both natural and common for people saved through the ministry of a particular worker to feel that they belong to that worker, and/or to that man's work or movement.

Unfortunately, Christian workers have the same concept. "I have led you to Christ; you belong to my work."

It may be natural for these attitudes to surface, it may even be common, but it is not spiritual. *It is contrary to God's will.* Nonetheless, many of God's servants have not realized this.*

No, division is not on the ground of one's instrument of salvation.

## Non-Sectarianism

There were Christians in Corinth who would have nothing to do with the sectarian attitude of "I am of Peter" and "I am of Paul" and "I am of Apollos." They stood up and proclaimed "I am of Christ." These were people who were looking down at the sectoring off that the other Christians were doing. Their attitude was, "You are sectarian and I am not sectarian. You are worshipers of human beings, but I worship the Lord alone." It does not take a very large step to go from there to saying, "Because you are sectarian and I am not sectarian, *I will separate from you. I* will do so on the ground that I am *not* sectarian and you *are* sectarian."

Those who were claiming that they were *of Christ* were also demonstrating a divisive spirit.

Of course it is not wrong to reckon yourself as belonging only to Christ. This is right and this is essential. It is not wrong to repudiate all schism. We must all repudiate the schisms which exist among the children of God. It is highly commendable to do so. God does not condemn a Christian for these matters. What is *not* proper here is that these people *condemn* the other believers for their sectari-

---

*Editor's Note: *All workers are servants of a visible, attendable, observable church!* There are not some servants who receive some *unique* call to some "universal" church that is unfindable. Nor are we called as workers to serve some private church or specialized organization that is not a church.

The church comes *before* the worker. The worker serves a geographically locatable, physical, visible, gathered, attendable, observable body of believers. Nothing else.

anism. This attitude is rampant today.

There are those who seek to divide themselves from other believers because "we are not divisive." (Those who divide from those who are divisive!) This ground of division may be more plausible than that of others who divide on the ground of doctrinal differences or personal preferences of leaders; nonetheless, the fact remains that they are dividing the children of God. Even while this believer repudiates all schisms, he creates a schism himself.

When you say "I am of Christ," do you mean to say that others might not be? It is perfectly fine to say that you are of Christ if you merely mean you belong to Him.

If you imply that you are not sectarian, and that you stand as different from the sectarian ones, you are making yourself different from other believers. You are distinguishing between the children of God, and this distinguishing between the Lord's people springs from a fleshly nature; it is in itself sectarian.

If you look at other believers and see them as sectarian and consider yourself to be non-sectarian, you have immediately made a differentiation between God's people. You are manifesting a divisive spirit even as you condemn division. It does not matter by what means you distinguish between members of the family of God; even if it be on the pretext of Christ himself, you are guilty of schism.

## We Must Cease All Distinctions Between Believers

Let us say that all exclusiveness is wrong. Let us say all inclusiveness is right. Let us say denominations are not scriptural and we are to have no part of them. But if we adopt an attitude of criticism, and think to ourselves, "They are denominational, I am undenominational; they belong to a sect, I belong to Christ alone"—such differentiation is definitely sectarian.

Yes, praise God, I am of Christ; but my fellowship is

not merely with those who say "I am of Christ." My fellowship is with all who *are* of Christ!

What is important is not the confession but the fact. A believer may say "I am of Paul." But the immovable truth is: He is not of Paul, he is of Christ. I overlook what this man says and I see what he is. He is of Christ.

I do not ask another believer if he is denominational or undenominational, sectarian or nonsectarian. I only inquire one thing, "Are you of Christ?" If that person is of Christ, then he is my brother. You should not denominate yourself, *but your fellowship should not be just with those who do not denominate themselves.* You should be nonsectarian, *but* you do not dare to fellowship only with those who are not sectarian.

That concept should never be established as a condition of fellowship. There is only one ground of fellowship between Christians. It is Christ Himself. Our fellowship should be with all believers who live *where we live.* If you move, the same is true there. You do not confine your fellowship to unsectarian believers in any situation.

Others may denominate themselves and make denominational differences. They may make denominating a requirement for oneness. But you must be careful to never make undenominating a requirement for fellowship. You dare not differentiate between yourself and another. Just because someone else differentiates between two Christians or groups does not mean you do. They are the children of God.

If some of the children of God distinguish themselves as different from other children of God, that does not cause them to stop being people of God!

A local body of believers in a city is undenominational, yet a so-called undenominational church *is* denominational; that is, it is denominating itself. The "church in Corinth" is scriptural, but the church of all those who say "I am of Christ" in Corinth is unscriptural.

If we come to a place where Christ is unknown, we must preach the gospel and win men and women to the Lord; and there, in that city, we must gather as the church. If we come to a place where there are already Christians but they are separated into denominational churches, our task is just the same as it was in the other place. We must preach the gospel, lead men to Christ and gather as the church. We must gather only on the ground that all Christians in that city are one with one another. We must maintain an attitude of *in*clusiveness, not exclusiveness. All believers within that place are one with one another. We must so walk.

It is not a matter of what we believe, it is not on peripheral doctrinal matters, it is not a matter of denominational, interdenominational, nondenominational, or undenominational; it is simply the fact that all believers in one geographical location are one with one another.

It is not our business to get people to leave sects and denominations. Let us make it our chief concern to lead people to a real knowledge of the Lord Jesus Christ and the power of His cross. If we do this, then others will gladly abandon themselves to Him. They will learn to walk in the Spirit and they will repudiate the things of the flesh. If we are faithful in showing them the Lord Jesus and the cross, then we shall find that there is no need to stress the question of denominating. The Spirit Himself will enlighten them. But if a believer has not learned the way of the cross and if he has not learned to walk in the Spirit, what is gained by his coming out of a sect?

### Doctrinal Differences

Paul shows us in Romans 14 how to deal with those whose views differ from ours, even though we may both be members of the church that is in that city.

What would you do if you were a believer in a city, began gathering with the church there, and then found that the church was a vegetarian church? That was somewhat the situation Paul was addressing. Please notice that he had a name for this business of debating over what day to observe and what food to eat. He called these debates "doubtful disputations" (verse 1). And that is what they are. He goes on to say:

> Who are you to judge a servant who belongs to another master? That servant stands or falls according to his Lord, not according to you. He will be made to stand; for the Lord has power to make him stand. (verse 4)
>
> Let us not judge one another any more, but rather judge this: that no man put a stumbling block in his brother's way. Let no man be a cause for another's falling. (verse 13)

Oh, for this largeness of heart. Alas, so many of God's children are so zealous for their pet doctrines that they immediately label another person a heretic and treat him like a heretic because that person's interpretation of some Scripture differs from his own. God would have us *walk in love* toward all who hold contrary views to those which we hold. (verse 15)

We must not form separate parties within the church, parties that reflect the different views that are held by different members of the body. Rather, walk in love toward those who have a different outlook from your own. We are to help *all* to come to the unity of the faith. (Eph.4:13)

As we wait patiently on the Lord, He may grant grace to others to change their views, or He may grant you grace to see that you are not such a good teacher as you might have thought you were.

*Nothing so tests the spirituality of one who teaches as does opposition to his teaching.*

If you would teach, then you must learn humility. So must all the other believers. But if you are to teach, you must also be willing to lay down your position as a teacher,...for it is by losing that we gain.

> Fulfill my joy, be of the same mind, have the same love, be of one accord, be of one mind; do nothing through faction or for vain glory, but in lowliness of mind, each of you count the other person better than you are. Do not look to those things which are yours, but look also to those things that are of others. (Phil. 2:2-4)

When a church has taken to heart what Paul wrote to the church in Philippi, then it will be perfectly possible to have one church in one place,...in oneness! A church with no faction whatever among its many members!

**Differences of Race**

Jews have always had the strongest racial prejudices of any people. They regard other nations as unclean. Jews were forbidden even to eat with other races. But Paul made it very clear in writing to the Corinthians that, *in the church,* both the Jew and the Gentile are *one*.

> For in one Spirit were we all baptized into one body, whether Jews or Greeks, whether slaves or free, and we were all made to drink of one Spirit. (1 Cor.12:13)

All the distinctions that existed "in Adam" are done away with when it happens that we come to be "in Christ." *A racial "church" has no recognition in the Word of God. Church membership is determined by domicile, not by race.*

Across the world, especially in large cities, you will find churches that are just for white people and others that are just for blacks. There are also churches for Europeans and churches for Asians. These churches have originated because of God's people's failure to understand that there is "the church in Rome," "the church in Ephesus," "the church in London," "the church in Johannesburg," "the church in Cape Town," "the church in Tel Aviv," "the church in Jerusalem," "the church in New York or Miami," but no church for skin colors! When God looks down upon those cities, He sees that every believer in a city, regardless of race and regardless of color, all belong to the church in that city. God does not permit division of His children on the ground of color or race any more than He does for custom, culture, or peculiarities in way of living.

*No matter what race you belong to, if you find yourself in the same place where there are other believers, then you belong to the same church they belong to.* No matter who they are, no matter who you are.

God has placed believers of different races in one location so that, by transcending all external differences, they would show forth the one life and the one Spirit of His Son.

All that we happen to be by nature is overcome by *grace!* Everything that belonged to you "in Adam" was ruled out when you were placed "in Christ."

The whole matter lies here: Are our carnal differences done away with in Christ? Or is there still a place for the flesh in the church? Are your resources and my resources in Christ sufficient to overcome natural barriers?

Always remember: The church in any place includes *all* the believers living within that place.

## National Differences

The difference between a Jew and a Gentile was racial, but there was also a matter of different nations. In the church of God we are plainly told that there is no such thing as a Hebrew or a Greek...that there are no racial distinctions...so also there are no national distinctions. No matter what your nationality, whether you have come into the city where you live as a foreigner or whether you were born in that city, *everyone* within that city belongs together in the body of Christ.

Yes, in the natural realm there is a difference between Chinese, French, English, Mexican, Nigerian and American; but in the spiritual realm *there are no differences*. If a Chinese lives in Nanking, he belongs to the church in Nanking. If a French believer lives in Nanking, he also belongs to the church in Nanking. The same holds also for a Britisher or an American or any other nationality. The only provision is that he must be redeemed by Christ.

In the Scripture we see "the church in Rome" recognized. We see "the church in Ephesus" recognized, and "the church in Thessalonica" recognized. However, we do not see a Jewish church, a Chinese church, an Italian church, nor a Greek church.

Why is it that each church was named after the city where the believers met? It is because difference in dwelling places is the *only* difference recognized by God among His children. Space and time separate us, nothing else does. The life in you and the life in me is essentially *one;* therefore, we are indivisible.

What happens if someone moves from one city to another? Once he arrives he is immediately a member of the church in that place.

There is no such thing as an extra-territorial church! The brother who is Chinese moves from Nanking to Chicago; he is now a member of the church in Chicago. If a British brother moves from London to Shanghai, he is immediately a member of the body of Christ in Shanghai. Nationality has no effect on membership in the body of Christ.

If a brother leaves China and goes to the South Sea Islands, he must not form an "overseas Chinese church" in those islands. You may have an overseas Chinese Chamber of Commerce or an overseas Chinese college or an overseas Chinese club. Anything you wish can be "overseas Chinese" with one exception: *the church.* There is *nothing* Chinese about the churches of God.

*How glorious it would be if all the believers, in every city, would overlook their natural, external and mental differences and consider their spiritual oneness.*

Whether or not Christ is in you determines whether or not you belong to the church. And to which church do you belong? To the one where you live! To that church which is in your city.

The question put by God to those who belong to the world is: "Do you belong to Christ?" The question put to those who belong to Christ is "Where do you live?" It is a question of *geographic domicile!*

The church of God knows neither Jew nor Greek; therefore, it knows neither native nor foreign, neither heathen country or Christian country. And if there is a Chinese worker and a foreign worker in a city in China, then we must make no difference between the Chinese worker and the foreign worker.

There is no church of the Gentiles in the Scripture. But we do read that there is a church of the Thessalonians! There should be no distinction between the nationality of one person and the nationality of another person, or the nationality of one Christian worker and the nationality of another worker. Neither should there be a difference, by the way, between the money given by a person of one nationality and money given by a person of another nationality!

## Social Distinctions

Socially, there is a great gulf between a free man and a slave. Yet, in the first Christian century, they were there worshiping side by side in the same gathering. In our day, if a rickshaw driver and the president of our country both live in the same city and both belong to Christ, then they belong to the same church.

Someone may wish to start a *mission* for rickshaw coolies, but no one must ever start a church for rickshaw coolies. *Social distinctions are not an adequate basis for forming a separate church.*

In the church of the living God there is "neither bond nor free."

* * *

So we see in the Scripture at least seven definite things referred to which are forbidden by God as reasons for dividing His church. These seven points are only typical of all the other reasons humans have come up with as excuses for dividing the church of God. In the two thousand years of church history, we see a sad record of human inventions and excuses that allow men to destroy the church's unity.

# 19

# What Do You Do if You Are Displeased with the Church?

If the spiritual life of a church is very low, can a few of the more spiritual members gather and form another assembly of the body of Christ?

Lack of spirituality is no adequate reason for dividing the church. The church may be far from ideal; that still constitutes no reason for division. Even wrong teaching is no ground for those who have a better understanding of doctrine to form a separate church.*

Ground for division is virtually nonexistent. If I am dissatisfied with the church where I gather, the only thing I can do is change my residence to another city! I will then automatically change the church I gather with! There is no other escape.

It is possible for you to leave a denomination. It is not possible for you to leave the church. To leave a church, whether on the ground of unspirituality, wrong doctrine, or bad organization, is utterly unjustifiable. If you form a separate assembly, you may have greater spirituality, purer teaching and better government; but you have no church, you have only a sect.

Consider this. The book of Revelation shows you

---

*In 2 John 9 you find an exception to this.

seven different cities. And there are also seven churches, but *only* seven. Seven cities, seven churches. Five of those churches were censured by the Lord Himself. Spiritually, those five churches were in a sad state. Those five churches were weak and defeated. But for all of that, they were all *still* churches. They were not sects, they were churches. Spiritually, they were wrong, *but that did not make any of them cease to be a church.*

What did God say to those who found themselves in a weak church? He said: "Be an overcomer." He did not say leave; He said, "Be an overcomer." By its very constitution, a church is not something you leave; you remain in it and with it. If you are more spiritual than the others present, then you should use your spiritual influence to revive that church. If the church does not respond, you have only two alternatives: (1) you must either remain there, keeping yourself undefiled and uncontentious; or (2) you must move to another city.

However weak any one of those five churches may have been, they were still the body of Christ in that city.

You will not find any place within the Scripture where anyone is authorized to leave the church and to divide himself from a church. You and I simply cannot cut ourselves off from other members of the body of Christ.

It is never right to leave a church while still living in the same town. If you do, then you do so without the authority of the Lord. If you do so, you become guilty of the sin of schism in the body of Christ. You have divided Christ himself.

What a tragedy when a few spiritual members leave a church and form another gathering simply because the members are weak and immature. Strong members should remain in the church and take the position of the call which God has given them, to be an overcomer. Seek to help weaker brothers and sisters. Claim the situation there for the Lord.

*How prone we are to despise believers whom we consider to be inferior to us spiritually!*

How we delight to associate with those whose fellowship we find congenial. This comes from pride of heart and a selfish desire to enjoy spiritual things. This pride of heart causes us to overlook the fact that the church consists of all the family of God within that place. We tend to narrow down Christian fellowship and make selections among the children of God. This is sectarian and it is a grief to the heart of the Lord.

However spiritual and strong any believer or church fellowship may be, there is no finer claim a company of Christians can make than "We are the believers in Christ in such-and-such a place."

# Part III

## Gene Edwards

# 20
# Facing Some Hard Realities

You have read Kokichi Kurosaki's *Let's Return to Christian Unity,* and now in this book you have heard from Warren Litzman and Watchman Nee. All three men call for a return to a visible unity in the body of Christ.*

I would like to begin my part of this book by looking at some harsh realities, and then some practical solutions.

Let us establish this: Through the eyes of God, the church is one—always has been, always will be—both universally and in the town you live in. But that is the view seen through the eyes of God. What about the eyes of those of us down here? What we see is a bit different. The unbeliever, for instance, sees us divided. And the believers?

Most Christians also see us divided. And they are going to continue to see the situation that way. Furthermore, it appears that we who are down here are going to *continue dividing!* Strange, is it not: So many of us *want* to see things as they are seen through the eyes of God and to experience our oneness with all others of God's people,

---

**Let's Return to Christian Unity* is part one of this two-book series on church unity, and is published by The SeedSowers—Christian Books Publishing House, Auburn, Maine.

yet the practice eludes us.

Can we expect a large number of the redeemed to behold things as they really are,...that is, as God sees them? Not likely. Not anytime soon, at least. But *yes*...in the future. Definitely, yes! Right now a great deal of that visionary hope may rest on how you and I—today—conduct ourselves. A strong and *pure* witness to unity is needed on this earth...desperately...and needed *now*. Please note the emphasis is on the word *pure*, as opposed to using unity as a gimmick to enlist people in a movement.

Is a strong witness to a practical unity possible, despite the cataclysmic and catastrophic failures of the past?

Yes, such a thing is possible.

As a first step, let's find out how we got in this mess in the first place.

# 21
# The Birth of a Curse

We begin with a little-known piece of history. A surprising piece of history, in fact, if not downright shocking. Here is the setting.

From A.D. 30 to about A.D. 327, the church had pretty well remained *one,* both universally and locally.*

But then along came Constantine, who called for a conference of Christian leaders near the capital city of *Constantinople.* (Constantine modestly had the capital of the western world named after himself.)

The reason for this conference? Some of the philosophers-turned-Christian had begun fighting among themselves over scriptural interpretations. Back home, in villages and farms across the known world, the ordinary members of the body were not even noticing the disputes any more than they would notice Constantine's conference. Unfortunately, Constantine saw these disagreements as quite threatening. He had never liked political or economic or military disharmony; and he did not like disharmony among so-called Christian leaders, either.

Constantine wanted the fighting to stop... not for the sake of brotherly love, but so that things could be better or-

---

*This author knows of but one major division during this time, the Donatist schism.

ganized; and then the church could more easily be set into the structure of the Empire. His was a demand for *mental* unity. Agreement of brains.

Constantine wanted a universal pledge drawn up which all Christians would agree to...even *swear* to. He wanted this agreement in writing. Therefore, he called for a gathering of Christian leaders, with the idea that if he could get them together they would come up with, and *sign,* a universally accepted pledge to common ideas.

Constantine's concept of unity was the reflection of a pagan mind. (Constantine may or may not have been a regenerated Christian, but he still had the mind of a pagan.)

*And here is that little-known historical fact:* Constantine brought with him to that meeting an entourage of heathen philosophers. He brought these men to a *Christian* gathering so they could help the Christians draw up the pledge and put the wording of that pledge in high-sounding philosophical terms.

These Greco-Roman philosophers, heathen to the core, sat in on that Christian conference and listened to the philosophers-turned-Christian debate their spiritual differences. When Constantine called for an end to this and called for drawing up the pledge (to be universally accepted by all Christians), the heathen philosophers aided in delineating the lines of agreement and in formulating the proper language for this pledge.

When the conference was over, Constantine demanded that all agree and sign. Most did. The Emperor *thought* he had succeeded in bringing objective, *surface* unity to Christendom. He had, in fact, done more than any another human in history to *guarantee* division!

By his actions, Constantine gave the Christian faith one of the *two* greatest *curses* ever to be brought into the Christian family. He gave us *theology!*

Theology was born at that conference. Theology is but

the philosophical mind-set invading the perimeter of religion. Or, in the case of Christianity, theology is but the philosophical mind-set dealing with the Christian faith. We will call this *Curse Number One*.

We have now lived with this damnable curse for seventeen hundred years. Since that hour, the Holy Scripture has been approached as a riddle—a theological puzzle to be unraveled—rather than the vibrant record of men who penned their words in the midst of a dynamic, living faith.

Oh, by the way, that conference came to be known as a *council*. This pledge, partly the work of cranial-heavy *heathen*, came to be known as the Nicene Creed.

Read it and weep. Our task? To undo that which really cannot be undone.

Let us wipe away our tears and see what happened next.

### The Aftermath

A great deal happened during the one hundred and fifty years that followed. At first Christianity was designated as *one* of the religions that was approved by the department of religion of the Empire. Evidently, however, all other religions were *disapproved*. The department of religion not only decided to sanction just one religion, the tax money allocated to the department of religion was all channeled to Christianity. Then came the golden rule:

*He who has the gold*
*makes the rules*.

Power now resided in simple followers of the Nazarene. The vacuum left by the empire's having but one official religion was soon filled. There was a vast numerical shift to where lay the power and the gold. Heathen flooded into the church...most of them utterly unconverted either in soul or mind. That, however, is but an infinitely small tragedy compared to the birth of Curse Number *Two!*

## Introduction to Curse Number Two

In the process of Christianity's becoming the only religion in the entire department of religion, and with the resultant influx of millions of unconverted "converts," a foreign (and decidedly unchristian) mind-set slipped into our faith. That mind-set has remained among us ever since and is daily working its damnation and destruction.

I refer to Curse Number Two, a curse so subtle it is almost imperceptible. And it might also be known as the invisible, or *unknown* curse. Nonetheless, this neo-pagan mind-set and the second curse that came with it have caused the death of untold scores of millions of Christians and wreaked tragedy, pain and heartache in the lives of all saints... including you and including me.

What is that mind-set? What is that curse? And how did it get into our bloodstream? To trace its origins and to fully understand this curse, let us begin with "the Fathers."

# 22
# The Fathers

To most Christians (in the organized church, at least) the names of Ambrose, Jerome, Dominic and Augustine—and others of their era—are the names of giants of the faith.

I beg to differ. Titanic minds, yes. Excellent philosophers, yes. But a friend of Christian unity, *no*.

A series of men, living between the years 323 and 500 A.D., brought so much hurt and harm to the faith that it is incalculable. These men were all heathen philosophers turned Christian. These are the philosophers/theologians who *wrote* during that period from Constantine until the disintegration of the Roman Empire in about 500 A.D.

Still later the Empire fragmented. With this fragmentation of the Empire came disintegration of travel, commerce and virtually all socio-economic intercourse between regions and cultures. Roads and bridges decayed and disappeared. International trade almost came to a halt. Education and knowledge eclipsed.

And somewhere in all that morass, someone got the idea that all final truth had been *stated* during the golden age of philosophy and theology (from Socrates to Gregory—200 B.C. to 500 A.D.). That seven-hundred-year period of time came to be known, loosely, as the *classical* period.

For Christians, the idea that *all* great thought had been stated during this period simply meant you had to believe *everything* the pre-Nicene and post-Nicene "fathers" wrote. If you were a thinker, you had to conceive thoughts along the schematic of Aristotle's rules for reasoning; if an artist, you had to paint by the philosophic concepts of the classics. If you were a physician, you dared not question what had been written during that time period. So also architecture, science, elocution, philosophy, and (shudder) theology.

Progress in science in Europe virtually died. So, too, medicine. Theology froze.

And so it came to pass that every comment the "fathers" made, no matter how off-the-cuff the remark, was analyzed to the *nth* and became church dogma.

To illustrate, Augustine said:

> "If a man forces you to believe in Jesus Christ, you should be grateful to him."

On the surface it would seem to be a *fairly* innocent statement—a wrong statement, yes, but fairly innocent. Nonetheless, that one comment by Augustine has caused the brutal, savage, torturous death of tens of millions of believers outside the organized church. People who refused to believe church dogma were burned at the stake, tortured in a contraption called "the iron virgin," slowly roasted alive, had their eyes gouged out or their leg tendons severed, body cavities had hot pokers shoved into them, and women in labor had their hips and legs tied together. And those who did these things claimed to do it in the name of, and by permission of, a comment by Augustine.

Consequently, one dared not disagree with the church's dogmatic interpretations of "the fathers"!

### From 500 A.D. to 1517 A.D.

Gradually the continent of Europe began to pull out of

its age of darkness—but not without the burning of a goodly number of scientists, medical doctors and astronomers, not to mention a large number of religious wars and burning of books on science, medicine and literature. Likewise, the church slaughtered a good number of heretics (some real, most imagined) on its way back to enlightenment.

During this time all the wise men of that millennium agreed that "the fathers" contained all truth. But they had a problem. Their problem was that they could not agree among themselves on the proper interpretations of what the *fathers* had said! Consequently, a lot of books were written, bonfires built, stakes employed, wars fought and blood shed over differences of opinion on the doctrines of the fathers.

The roots of all this horror began with Constantine, at Nicene.

(Today would we make these terrible mistakes? Would you? Please wait just a little while before you answer. You might surprise yourself.)

Finally came the Renaissance and the Reformation. But, alas, Curse Number Two was still hard at work during the Reformation. In fact, the Reformation was about to give Curse Number Two its best days.

# 23
# The Reformation and Curse Number Two

Luther, Calvin, Zwingli, Erasmus, the popes, etc. really showed us the power of Curse Number Two in stark relief during these days. There were more wars, more books, more debates, more burnings, and more and more division. Protestants, it seemed, could not abide one another any better than Catholics could abide heretics. Unless they agreed with each other on *every* point of theology, Protestants fought. They fought literally and physically.

And just what is Curse Number Two? Whatever it is, it is the mind-set of *every* Protestant and every Catholic, and yes, every Pentecostal and every fundamentalist *and all* the rest of us evangelicals. This curse is in our blood and in our bones. It is part of our neurons (and sub-particles) that make up the atoms in our brains.

The curse?

> "If I have the best interpretation of Scripture—if I understand Scripture best—God stands with me the most."
>
> Or
>
> "Your theology is what causes God to decide to come over and stand with you and your group, or to *not* stand with you. He likes you best if you understand best what it is *God* believes."

Or

"Wrong theology, God no like you.
Good theology, God like you.
Perfect theology, God come live with you...

*And*

"He no like anyone else but *you!!*"

*That* is Curse Number Two! Ever see it at work?

The Catholic church dominated Europe from 500 to 1517 A.D. During that time only a few brave souls bucked the accepted trends... at risk of life and limb. Nonetheless, Curse Number Two had plenty of space to operate in during that time. Curse Number Two, at that time, looked like this:

> "Catholic theology is best. God stands with us because our theology matches God's. God likes us for that reason. If you don't believe our theology, we will simply burn you at the stake."

During this period there was not only fighting in western Europe among Catholics and heretics, but also there was a great split between the Orthodox church of the east and the Catholic church of the west. And yes, that caused wars and bonfires. There were also fights between religious orders, and then there was the Abelard controversy, Joan of Arc's trial and burning, the burning of Huss, the war between the Hussites and the rest of Europe, the Albigensian crusade, and the persecution of the Nestorians and Manicheans.

Within the church itself, there were theologians throwing anathemas at one another and appealing to the pope to burn the other fellow,...quick! (See Molinos and the Jesuits; Bossuet and Fenelon, as examples.)

Even Thomas Aquinas got in trouble with his writings until the pope sided with him. Not to mention the trouble that Copernicus and Galileo got into for just looking at stars. Columbus was once even threatened with the stake for promulgating the teaching that the world was not flat, in opposition to the teaching of the church.

*All* of this was simply Curse Number Two hard at work:

> "God sides with those people who have best figured out God's theology."

Enter Luther, Calvin, Zwingli, etc.

The day Protestantism was born, the mind-set, "God is first and foremost a theologian who is looking for the fellow with the best and most correct theology to match His," came with it.

The Reformation was neither *revival* nor restoration. The Reformation was an intellectual brawl. All Protestants would have nothing to do with Catholics. Then they looked at one another and would have nothing to do with one another because dots on "i's" were a bit off-center.

The fury and vengefulness with which a man will stand for his theological convictions—despite how appalling and catastrophic the consequences—is now in the very bloodstream and marrow of *all* Protestantism. Yes, *even* today!

Underlying the whole Protestant subterranean structure is that deep, unconscious idea that God will go over and bless the group that best figures out what God believes; and He will have little or nothing to do with a man (or a people) who is off a little here and there.

The polar star of Protestantism, like Catholicism, *today* is nothing less than that curse:

> "My beliefs are closer to God's theology than yours, and though you are a fellow believer in Christ, that fact counts for *nothing*... I am closer to God's own personal theology than you. God likes me best. I will have absolutely nothing to do

> with you, and I doubt God does. Repent of your theological teachings, come over here where God likes best, and I'll touch you. But *not* until then. Forget the fact that Christ died for you and for me and that He has received us both. What is actually important is *my* theology. Accept it, or I will forever hold you at arm's length."

*We who are about to kill one another pause before the blood letting to profess the name of Jesus!*

You would never be such a Christian as that, would you?

(Don't bet on it.)

Dear saints of God, this attitude toward God and theology *must* be abandoned! Given up! Forsworn. Forsaken. Doubtful disputings over doubtful doctrines must not, in any way, come between believers or build *any kind* of walls.

I once heard a dear saint asked, "Brother, why do Christians divide so much?"

His answer was shocking.

"Because we love God so much."

His words are true. "I love God too much to run around with people who believe the kind of error you do."

"You love God so much you will do everything in your power to stop me!"

Do you love God *that* much?

Let's see how much our more recent forefathers loved one another.

### Baptists, Methodists, etc.

After Luther, Calvin and other assorted reformers fought one another for centuries, and after the English had it out with the Italians, and the Scots had it out with the English, along came the *free churches*.

Baptists and Methodists have axed one another (figuratively speaking) for two hundred years. The Campbellites threw damnations at everyone. And all the other "free church" denominations more or less do the same. Why? Because those who have pigeon-holed the best theology, *they* are those whom God likes best. "*We* have the best theology. Come embrace us or we will have nothing to do with you... not to mention the fact that God likes our theology best."

How deep runs this curse in our veins?

I come from the Southern Baptist branch of the tree. I have sat in our two-thousand-seat auditorium at the seminary I attended and watched two thousand students applaud wildly as the speaker of the day vaunted Baptist theology and impaled the theologies of everyone else. That heady stuff gets in your bloodstream. You doubt? Then go talk to a good Southern Baptist.

I have also sat in a Methodist conference where the speaker shook his finger directly at me and told me that my theology was of the devil and belonged in the pit of hell!

About half the books in *any* denomination's seminary library are attacks on someone else's beliefs.

I was stopped in the street by a Christian one evening and told I was *not* a brother because I did not believe the way *he* did.

This doesn't stop with denominations. There is an independent seminary down in Texas that makes its students sign a pledge that says, essentially: I believe in dispensational premillennianism. If I ever give up this view I will leave the ministry and never preach again.

And there is an interdenominational organization that has a rule that goes something like this: If you have ever spoken in tongues you may not join this organization. And if you ever do, you have to leave.

It gets worse.

The "closed" Plymouth Brethren will have nothing to

do with the "open" Plymouth Brethren. And if someone who is a member of a "closed" church should happen to have *any* fellowship with someone who belongs to an "open" church, the entire "closed" church where he meets is ruled "unclean."

And think! They all will quote the Bible to you to prove these practices to be *scriptural*.

You wouldn't do that, would you?

I was invited to speak in someone's home in Florida one night and, being less than sagacious, I accepted. I made the very *big* mistake of observing, off-handedly, the need to return to Christian unity. Well, seventeen hundred years of doctrinal differences suddenly surfaced. I genuinely thought the whole meeting was about to end in fisticuffs.

As I watched this bizarre scene, what fascinated me the most was an older gentleman who began to lecture us all on a verse in Ezekiel. I had no recollection of anything central to the Christian faith mentioned in the chapter he referred to, and I had never even heard the verse he referred to! But never in my life had I ever seen *anyone* so obsessed with the conviction that it was an absolute necessity for *all* of us to see that verse the way he did and that everything that had to do with the kingdom of God hung on that verse and his interpretation thereof.

You would never be that adamant, would you?

Now I come to the point. With Curse Number Two so hard at work, this question begs for an answer: Will all the aforementioned groups *ever* cease their separation?

**Not Likely!**

Baptists and Campbellites *cannot* become one. Why? The engine that fuels those two movements is their *beliefs*. Take away their doctrines and both those movements lose their momentum, and perhaps even their main reason for existence.

But there is a far larger reason than theology lurking in the shadows that will forever keep most denominations from laying down their walls of separation. That reason emerged into stark daylight during the heyday of...

**The Ecumenical Movement**

The years of the 1930's, '40's and '50's were the golden years of the ecumenical movement. Several denominations did join one another. They had problems in so doing, but you probably cannot guess what those problems were. When it came down to unifying denominations, it turned out that it was not theology after all that caused the smoke and fire. The fights were over *salaries* and *titles*. Money and power. And, please note, the ecumenical movement is not a return to unity of the body of Christ; it is only an organizational unity.

When two ecumenically-minded denominations begin talking merger, the sticky part is still money, power and fame. Income, prestige, honor.

Separation between Christians has always had its taproot *here*.

And if you don't think so, watch what will happen if you ever hear that *one* Baptist pastor and *one* Campbellite minister are trying to merge their two fellowships into one. Denominational powers will fall on both those men. Why? Because of land, buildings and money. And *both* pastors know that fact. And *that* is why you will *never* hear of a merger between two such churches.

Money, power and prestige are what keep us separated. Plus, of course, our absolute assurance that God takes sides according to exactitudes of doctrines, teachings and theology.

Will that religious organization which tells a tongue-talking charismatic he cannot join their movement ever let charismatics in? Not likely. Maybe the day after the Second Coming. Furthermore, theology is *not* the reason they exclude charismatics. Here is the reason: A large part of the money that comes in to the coffers of that particular organization comes from churches that teach that tongues are of the devil, or (at least) not scriptural. *That is* really why charismatics cannot go on staff with that organization. Money would decrease.

(Money, power, prestige. The ingredients of virtually *all* division. Throw in personality clashes and you have it all, for these are the true ingredients which cause men to begin accusing other men of false doctrine.)

And will the Southern Baptist Convention ever merge with *anybody?* Not a chance. The entire fabric of the convention would disintegrate. We Southern Baptists have a sacred cow called the Cooperative Program. Nooobody had better ever question, or change, or place in jeopardy the Cooperative Program. Why? Well, that's a good question. But the answer is clear enough. Because the Cooperative Program furnishes the *salaries* of tens of thousands of people, that's why!

Point: It is highly unlikely that the religious system will *ever* father a return to Christian unity. Theology—and God's obvious blessing on whatever group gets it right—plus money, power and prestige will forever prevent oneness in the body...until the crack of doom.

Unless!

Unless God's people get enough of all this, and simply walk out.

# 24
# The Theological God

Let's take a moment and look at the God who sides with the best theology.

Let's gather up a few pictures to put in this scene.

Let's take wine, prayer, and the Second Coming and hold these up before a theological God. Here's why I have chosen these three points.

One day I was in a conference in Pasadena, California when someone asked me whether the group sponsoring the conference used wine or grape juice in the Lord's supper. I didn't know. He proceeded to explain that it had to be *wine*.

Foolishly, I asked if he would insist on that if a man was a reformed alcoholic who had vowed never to drink alcohol again. I ventured a few more dumb questions until it became apparent that this man saw all the kingdom of God pretty much hanging on wine! It had to be *wine*...regardless.

As a guest speaker one Sunday in Houston, Texas, I closed the morning service with a prayer. Immediately a man in the audience made a beeline for me. "You opened your prayer with, 'Dear Lord Jesus' and you did *not* end with 'in Jesus' name.'" He explained that a prayer had to begin addressed only to the Father, and *had* to end "in Jesus' name."

On another occasion I was with about a dozen men in a small retreat house near Lake Arrowhead in California. We were deep in a discussion on *body life*. Among us was a man who was destined to become one of the most influential premillennialists of all time. As we spoke together on the subject of church life, he inserted a comment about dispensational premillennianism, observing that there could be no return to true church life unless there was a commonly held view of premillennianism. I was struck by one sentence: "This is absolutely necessary."

All right, with those three anecdotes in mind, let's look at our theological God and wine, prayer, premillenianism, etc.

There He is, God (up in heaven) sitting in front of a vast computer console. Meanwhile, down in Louisiana, U.S.A. (or Liverpool, England) a prayer is prayed.

"Here it comes now," says our theological God.

"Hmmm. He prayed 'Dear Father.' For that he gets one point. He prayed 'in Jesus' name,' that's one point. Let's see, he's Armenian in his theology and can't stand Calvinistic doctrine, that's minus five points. But he was immersed when baptized; that's three points. He's never spoken in tongues; that's ten points. He's never given to the Cooperative Program; that's minus ten points. He tithes; one-half point. He gave extra money to an organization called *Winning-Men-with-Masters-Degrees-in-Science-to-Christ Crusade;* that's fifteen points! He failed to witness last week; minus one-eighth point. He prophesied in a meeting last Sunday; eight and three-quarters points. He listened to a radio program on family life; that's ten more points. He drinks wine at the Lord's Supper. Hmmm...that depends on how *much* he drinks. He home-schools his kids; that's seven points. He also sent in gifts to *five* TV evangelists; that's minus twenty points.

"Oh, but he's premillennial; that's ten points. He is dispensational premillennial; that's fifteen points. And he is even pre-tribulation; that's thirty points! What's this! He *hates* postmillennialists. That's five points. Ah, and he absolutely loathes amillennialists. That's good for *at least* one hundred points.

"I'm definitely going to answer his prayer!"

It is all kind of silly, isn't it? God isn't really like that, you know. And His value system of love toward you is not in any way attached to your doctrines. Isn't it about time we gave all this up?

And you? Well, if yours is a theological God, then your chance of experiencing the beauty of oneness with your brothers and sisters is a *minus zero.*

All of this denominating foolishness must go to the cross. And "all" means *all.*

By the way, what's that little doctrinal god you've got hiding back there behind you?

# 25
# Do Ordinary Christians Want Division?

Believers of the world, unite; you have nothing to lose but your differences.

Down deep, I don't think ninety per cent of the lay Christians in this world really care about all these terribly important differences between Christians. I have a theory. If all the clergy and theologues and Bible teachers suddenly disappeared from the earth, most of the church would be back to oneness in sight of six months.

I once knew an independent Baptist preacher in east Texas who never spoke to his people on any topic except *prophesy*. He also had a daily radio program in which he did the same. Nonetheless, with all that input he gave his congregation, I always had the distinct feeling his people could not have talked intelligently about the Lord's return for much longer than two minutes. His people really only understood this: "Whatever my pastor believes about this is all-important. He has the right view, and I find real personal significance and satisfaction in knowing I belong to the one group that has the right view on this all-important subject."

And what about us Southern Baptists? There is really only one thing holding us together: The Cooperative Program. There is not a single practice (or doctrine) which we *all* swear to—*just* the Cooperative Program. And yet

I've got money in my clothes that says ninety-nine per cent of God's people in the typical Baptist church could not give you *any* scriptural reason for the Cooperative Program, and ninety-five per cent would not be able to tell you what the Cooperative Program is. But boy, that doesn't stop them from being whole-heartedly committed to it!

My point? If all our much-respected leaders stopped speaking on doctrinal and organizational distinctions, the whole issue of division among ordinary believers would be forgotten in sight of two years.

Never forget this: Christians love to be with other Christians who love the Lord, regardless of stripe. (By the way, does a zebra have white stripes over black, or black stripes over white? Oh, I see! Your zebra is black with white stripes, but those miserable buzzards down the street have white zebras with black stripes!) Never forget: It scares the wallet out of preachers when they see their people joyously and wholeheartedly fellowshiping with anyone who belongs to the opposition.

And will denominations and nonprofit religious organizations stop emphasizing distinctions, differences and doctrines? Not likely. Probably not until money, power, prestige and doctrines disappear off the face of the earth.

In fact, today the very subject of *one body* in Christ is virtually never mentioned. It's a dead subject. Forgotten. Forgotten either because of its unimportance or its impossibility. It will become important, though, if you and a few hundred thousand other believers don't show up at your denominating gathering place.

*Denominations* will *never* be the prime movers in a return to Christian unity. Unity will *not* originate there. You might hear organizational unity spoken of within the ecumenical movement. But practical, spiritual, *divine* unity, down there on the grass-roots level...not likely. A return to unity will begin at the grass roots, among so-called "laymen," *or it will never come at all!*

Laymen of the world, walk out. You have nothing to lose, and perhaps you will gain the fellowship of tens of thousands of other believers.

If you let a premillennialist and an amillennialist meet together, would not the kingdom of God end, the world take over, and the devil rule heaven and earth forever and forever?

No?!

Well, for sure that would happen if non-tongue-talkers and tongue-talkers are allowed to be one with each other, with no boundaries of separation.

Do you really believe that?

## What About Heresy and Heretics?

But what about those rascals who do not believe in the Bible, the virgin birth, the resurrection of Christ, etc., etc.? How are we going to keep those heretics out if we don't emphasize doctrine?

I really hate to tell you what I am about to tell you.

Why?

Because I think of all the wasted effort out there that is being expended to "defend the faith." I think of all the radio programs with speakers warning us about *"all those evil heretics out there."* I think of the hundreds of thousands of lectures that will be given this year, all pointing out what heresy is and all warning you to *"be on guard against heretics."*

I think of all the books written that defend the Christian faith against heretical teaching. The volumes upon volumes of books, tapes, videos, radio programs, television programs, correspondence courses, etc. defending the virgin birth and warning you about all those zillions of people who don't believe in the resurrection.

Then I think, "I really hate to tell you what I'm going to tell you."

What is it? This:

*I've never met one!*

"You, Gene Edwards, have *never* met a heretic?!"

"In forty-two years in the ministry, I have never met a heretic."

"But what about all those Mormons?"

"I've never met one. Oh, they've come to my door, but that's about the limit of my contact with them."

"What about Jehovah's Witnesses?"

"Well, when I figure it's one of them at my door, I tell them I have the 'Blue Bonnet Plague' and I can't talk right now."

"Gene Edwards, you've never met anybody in all your life who denied the virgin birth and resurrection?"

"Well, no. Oh! Do atheists count? I've met a couple of them. They not only don't believe in the virgin birth... why... those folks don't even believe in God! *But they also don't come to any of our meetings, either!* Neither do Christian Scientists, Mormons or Jehovah's Witnesses come to our meetings."

And for those of you who are always trying to show proof of *creation* instead of *evolution;* and those of you who can deliver twenty-five red-hot lectures on "Why the Bible *Is* the Word of God"; and to you who have tapes, videos, charts and graphs *proving* that Jesus Christ rose from the dead... I've got something else to tell you:

> In all my ministry I have never met a
> believer who doubted the Bible, never met
> one who believed in Darwinian evolution,
> never met one who doubted the virgin birth,
> never met one who doubted the resurrection.
> No doubts at all...
>
> *until*
>
> he heard one of your lectures defending
> those things. *Then* he begins to doubt.

Believers not only don't doubt the tenets of the faith,

they never even think about doubting such things until someone tries to prove them to be true.

We are barking up the wrong tree when we try to keep believers from heresy. We expend an awful lot of energy trying to make sure saints don't go around denying Jesus' deity. Spending all that time convincing believers to believe what they already believe... that is not only barking up the wrong tree... that's barking up a tree that's not there.

Out here where I live, believers never dream of questioning the foundational tenets of the faith. Do you have a problem in this area? Do you live in fear of heretics? Many do. Outside the organized church, most believers never even hear of such things.

The same is true of the Lord's return. I've never met any professing believer who did not believe in the Lord's return. (Unfortunately, though, *how* He is going to return is a different matter. We hear alot about that, do we not? But that is a *man-made* problem which has no business separating us.)

If some of you fellows wouldn't be so dogmatic in your teachings of *how* He will return, God's people would be able to give one another a little space to believe a little differently from one another regarding the details of His return. But some of you have a few of God's people so convinced your view is the *only* view that they think anyone who sees it differently must be the devil's mother-in-law.

Believers being led into denying the fundamentals of the faith is a scenario I do not recall—in forty-two years as a minister—having *ever* encountered.

Do you know why we are called *believers?* It is because we believe. Believers believe!*

Let me reiterate two basic facts. "Lay-Christians" just

love to be with one another and simply do not care about all those precious doctrinal distinctions. They have to be placed under a lot of constant logic, dogmatism and pressure before they will pull away from other saints.

Stick to the message of Jesus Christ, back off from your "doubtful disputations," and God's people will move toward one another like hot syrup. And forget your fears about evangelical believers denying their faith. Believers don't do that. And if a few do, they are microscopic in number. So microscopic that I, for one, have never met any. People who hear the *glory* of Christ don't doubt their Lord, they *glory* in Him.

Our problem is not heresy, our problem is Christian workers who don't have the foggiest notion of how to make Jesus Christ central in all things. Rather than spending all that time, money and effort in disproving heresy, find someone who can raise up Christian workers who will know only Christ...and channel your time and efforts in *that* direction!

No, I've never met a believer in my entire life who had any problems with the cardinal principles of the faith. But I've met boatloads of believers who were rapaciously hungry to know their Lord better.

Will the institutional churches stop warning their people about the false doctrines and heresy of the folks in that church down the street? Will Jesus Christ become the centrality of the present-day expression of the church? Will laymen be left alone by their leaders to love one another? If not, is there hope for unity in the body of Christ? Where lies our hope?

---

*And if you think I live in Antarctica; I've spent half of my Christian life on the road...covering forty-nine of our fifty states, plus Guam and Midway Island. (And, yes, I'm making plans to go to Alaska to make it an even fifty.) There are about one hundred twenty nations on this planet, and I'm whittling away at visiting about one-third of those. Give it up. We believers are not heretics. It's a dead issue, friend. Believing is organic to our species! We *Believe!*

# 26
# Step One: Becoming Honest About Unity

The best hope for unity in the body of Christ has always resided outside the organized church. From about 365 A.D. to 1700 A.D., it was dangerous—even life-threatening—to be a believer outside the traditional church, but some dared! Integrity and grace under fire are their hallmarks.

Our best hope for a visible, observable display of the unity of Christ's body lies in the twenty-first century. *So let's get to it.* But as we do, even the folks outside the organized church have some housecleaning to do. There are some pretty sad-looking skeletons lying around in our closets, too. Here is one which we *need* to deal with.

### Curse Number Two and a Half

It was in the early 1800's that Christians outside the organized church got off track.

As the story goes, there was a Christian, a dentist,* who began a fellowship of believers in Ireland. He drew up a simple—and wonderful—statement about the body of Christ needing to be one, and included some guiding principles on how to achieve this. I doubt anyone has ever

---

*Anthony Norris Groves of Exeter, England, who was then studying at Trinity College in Ireland; he and a few others were meeting in the home of E.W. Hutchinson of Dublin.

improved on his words. The little group he started met around *the Lord.* Its numbers grew, and other groups meeting with the same heart began to form in other cities. Things were definitely looking up for the kingdom of God. One evening a Church of England clergyman, a Londoner serving in Ireland as an Anglican curate, joined one of these meetings. He later left the Church of England and eventually became the leader of the movement that had grown out of the dentist's little group. This clergyman led them (perhaps unwittingly) from being Christ-centered to being Bible-centered.

The man was John Darby. A more complex piece of machinery probably never existed. He was a man full of contradictions, with a personality so multi-faceted he is still not understood. Suffice it to say, he had a hard edge about him. John Darby's teachings are the warp and woof of today's fundamentalism; and the spirit of that hard edge still permeates the teachings, both among those whose movement he founded and among fundamentalists.

There is also the still-debated subject of just how truthful Darby was at certain times. To wit, when the Plymouth Brethren (which they later came to be called) began to fall under criticism, and words like "cult" were beginning to be thrown at them, they came up with a very effective answer to their critics,

> "We teach nothing but the Bible, only the Bible, and all the Bible. We preach only the *pure* Word of God."

They also added another statement, its veracity very much in question.

> "There have been no outside influences on us. No one has taught us these things. We learned *all* that we teach *only* from the Bible."

That last statement just doesn't wash with the facts.

Their Bible teachings were strongly peppered with opinions, reasonings, and giant leaps of logic. *And* the early founders of the Brethren had been greatly influenced by teachings of other men and other books.

From that day on, this business of playing loose with facts, while standing foursquare on the Bible, slipped into the bloodstream of many other groups outside the organized church. For the first time in church history, the integrity of groups outside the organized church began to erode. Over the years, playing fast and loose with claims and facts *became* one of the hallmarks of most groups *outside* the organized church.

Which brings us to Curse Number Two and a Half.

That dentist was a sincere man who wanted to have a place where all Christians of all backgrounds could come together on the common ground of Christ. Their call was *"unity without conformity"* and *"unity in diversity."* A large number of dear saints all over the British Isles responded to this wonderful call.

But somewhere along the way, this call for unity became *a method. A method used for growth.* An even better word than "method" is "gimmick." It was not long after Darby came along that *diversity without conformity* became just words. All Brethren were under extreme pressure to *conform* wholly to Darby's teaching. *That* is not diversity, and it *is* conformity.

Nonetheless, the original concept of unity had great appeal to saints, and their numbers grew.

So entered Curse Number Two and a Half...using the call for unity as a gimmick to start and to *grow* a movement. Other groups noticed the Brethren's growth *and* their sleight of hand. Other groups began to pick up on both!

This gimmick is still going strong today.

Here is that same curse at work in modern dress. See that innocent little group of believers meeting in that living room: They are as innocent—and dumb—as sheep can get.

In comes a visitor who offers a teaching.

> "The hour is dark. The end of the age is upon us. The church of Jesus Christ is about to enter awesome and grievous persecution. It is time for the Lord's people to fulfill our Lord's prayer as prayed in John, 'Father, make them one even as we are one.' Let us drop our differences and become one; then the Lord's prayer will be answered. Let us prepare ourselves for persecution and for the day when *all* believers will become one because of the grievous persecution."

Sounds fairly plausible. Except for one problem.

The fellow doing the talking is head of a nationwide *movement.* He is building a movement—maybe a denomination—using a call to unity in the body of Christ as his opening ploy. His movement is growing by *annexation.* They annex little house groups. And *major* conformity awaits those dear, innocent sheep who respond to this man.

A lot of groups outside the religious system have used, are using, and will continue to use this very unscrupulous tactic to add numbers to their movement. Those who are taken in by this appeal invariably end up in a movement that wields unbelievable control over the private lives of the people who belong to the movement. God's people, tragically, end up under pressure to conform. This pressure can get so intense it can quite literally create major health problems.

Scary, isn't it?

To put it another way, as long as Christian workers outside the organized church use a call for unity in the body of Christ as a means of growing up a movement, *then we will not see true unity blossom out here, outside the organized church, any more than we will see it within the organized church.*

There is a great deal of loss of integrity out here among Christians "outside the organized church." Repeat: Some major housecleaning is in order.

Most of the groups outside the organized church are strongly flavored with Darby-like fundamentalism and dispensational premillennianism. They also have a hard edge.

The *other* major group out here is Pentecostal/charismatics. By its very nature, the charismatic movement needs miracles, signs and wonders, every day, to fuel its engine. Consequently, Pentecostal/charismatics have always had a problem separating reality from fantasy, and truth from non-truth.

This is *not* an appealing scenario. At least not to me.

There are serious problems out here among too many groups who stand outside the religious system. These problems need to be delineated, defined, addressed, repented of, and some radical solutions implemented. Either that will happen *or* God's people, on their way to an expression of unity in His body, are going to reject this charade and leave these movements sitting in their gimmicks.

Having looked at this present mess, let's see if we can find a means to return to genuine unity in the body of Christ in the twenty-first century.

# 27
# Step Two: A New Breed of Workers

Church history records that Christians outside the organized church have always shied away from persecuting other Christians, have circumnavigated doctrinal issues, have been charitable to those who attacked them...and, in general, have walked with a spirit of love and forbearance toward all. At least, until recently.

There are still many today who walk in that wonderful witness. Nonetheless, the Plymouth Brethren of the early 1800's introduced a harsh, exclusive and elite spirit—not to mention their habit of playing loose with facts and making credal statements not totally in line with their practice. They did great damage to the witness and the testimony of Jesus Christ among believers *outside* the organized church.

Those of you who are reading these words, those of you who belong to the future, you must turn from these habits and return to that earlier stand of integrity.

Be certain: A more credible witness to Christ—outside the organized church—*will* emerge.

What, then, can you and I do—today—about the unity of the church?

### The Solution

The crux of the problem, from Constantine until this

good hour, has *never* lain with so-called laymen. The problem begins with, and is usually carried to its disastrous conclusion by, the Christian worker (that is, minister, pastor, preacher, administrator, church planter, organizational head, etc). Laymen often become pawns. And, yes, laymen even split churches; but someone usually had to get brainwashed, on some issue, first.

Our greatest need, therefore, is a new breed of worker. We need Christian workers who are committed to the oneness of the body of Christ above even life itself.

Raising up a new breed of workers will not be easy.

I would like to offer a description of this much-needed worker. What will characterize his attributes? And why do we need men of such caliber?

## Qualifications of the Future Worker

Needed: broken men. There must come upon the stage of church history a body of men—called of God—who are *broken* men. Men who can lose. Men who can fail. Men who will *never* fight to keep their ministry. Men not addicted to ministry. Men not tied to saving their work.

This takes strong men. Weak men run away under pressure. And *un*broken men fight. Broken men acquiesce, release their work, and go on to labor in other places.

Needed: Christ-centered men. Men who can stand on their feet and minister nothing but the Lord Jesus Christ for thirty years—every day. Men who can proclaim a living Christ. Men who speak of enduring the cross of Christ. Men who will, and men who *have,* surrendered the churches they have raised up; men who have relinquished those churches into the hands of others.

Men who can speak on the return of Jesus Christ with such descriptions of majesty and glory that your heart feels like it is going to burst—yet when they have finished you still don't know their eschatological theology.

Men who can speak on any scriptural subject without

indulging in exclusiveness or elitism. Men who never use the gimmick of "we are special." Men who declare that there is no difference—in God's eyes—between Christians in one group or another, nor among those in the traditional churches and those outside the organized church. Men who neither attack tongues nor demand them.

Men who have the whole world on their hearts, while not neglecting the need—nor overlooking the frailty—of the local gathering.

Men who, when they go to holy and inspired Scripture, see the centrality of Christ and not the centrality of the Bible.

Men who don't push, insist, adjust, or threaten; men who do not use fear in order to maintain position. Men who are not controllers, and men who are not legalistic. Men who stand in horror of putting God's people under the law.

Deeply spiritual men who strive to bring God's people to a meaningful walk with Christ. Men who, in every locale where they labor, labor to put themselves out of a job.

Such men do not exist. (If they do, they are doing a great job of staying hidden.) But one day they will exist.

Now, let me quickly add that when it comes to unity, even these lofty elements are worthless unless the next two ingredients are also present.

# 28
# The Christian Worker, Money, and Unity

Let's say it is Topeka, Kansas. Or Glasgow, Scotland. Or Debrecen, Hungary.

There is a group of believers meeting in a home on the east side of town. This group was brought into existence by a brother we will call Art Adams. On the other side of town is another group, raised up by Bill Brown. (Let's also say both these men have all the attributes of a worker listed in the previous chapter.)

Bill comes to visit his group once every six months; Art, once every four months.

Art is dependent on his group for part of his income; Bill is also dependent on his group for part of his income.

The two groups discover one another. (Both groups fit the description given in an earlier chapter of God's people and their desire to be one with other believers.)

Will these two groups become one? The chances are about the same as a prayer offered in hell.

Why? Well, certainly doctrine is not the reason.

Because both those men are *financially* dependent on the groups they minister to. History records only the rarest incidences when Christian workers give up their *incomes*. A person's income is simply one of the most powerful and influential forces in his life.

"But after the merger, couldn't both continue receiving financial help?"

Sure, if you can absolutely guarantee them ahead of time that it will happen that way...and that it will *stay* that way. No, there are too many unknowns, the situation is too risky. No one can guarantee the future, and *that* is why two groups rarely merge.

There is a solution. But this solution is revolutionary, and it is unknown in our age. And it is also unprecedented in modern church history.

> The solution is for church planters to *work for a living!* For Christian workers to *not* be dependent on the churches they raise up for their financial survival.

*That* is revolutionary. (It is also an *extremely* distasteful idea to Christian workers!) It is, nonetheless, one of the major keys to Christian unity. Without it we are in deep trouble.

For there to be unity in the body of Christ, there are going to have to be *some* men who have a passion for Christ and a passion for His church, who—for His sake and *her* sake—work for a living. They will do this for the sake of unity.

Unthinkable!

Yes, unthinkable, but necessary.

If those two Christian workers there in Topeka, Kansas, face no major financial loss in merging their two groups, the chances *are* good that the two groups will become *one!* And, in so doing, those two men will raise a witness to angels and men, a witness to Christ, to the cross, and to the oneness, in Christ, of believers...for all to see.

Without this new breed of worker there will probably never be a witness among God's people to unity.

And now, the *other* obstacle.

# 29
# The End of a Movement Mentality

If you belong to a movement of any kind, you can forget about seeing a practical expression of the unity of the body of Christ.

And, *no,* people do not have to end up being a movement.

Maybe I should define what a movement is. It is a number of Christians in several different places *who are acting together* toward a very large goal. That goal may be to evangelize campuses all over the world, to get people filled with the Holy Spirit, to evangelize the world in one generation, or even to plant a specific *kind* of church all over (1) the state, (2) the country, or (3) the world. These are *specialized* movements.

No such "movement" existed during the first century.

Specialized movements are an immeasurable distraction to unity in the body of Christ. To have a common objective is one thing; to *network* that objective is another. To have a common goal (and to be under pressure to reach that goal) is a built-in mechanism for distraction from Christ. *Failure* will be the best thing that such people can hope for. Let us hope, for the sake of the unity of the body of Christ, that they *do* fail.

(I often wonder: In God's eyes which is more important, the evangelization of the world, or unity of the body of Christ—doctrinal agreement, or unity in the body of Christ?)

Look for a moment at that movement right over there. They have *one thousand* churches! (That is too many.) Recently they set a goal to have *ten thousand* churches . . . in just ten years. (Why grow so fast? Why, don't you know: The Lord is coming back and we have to hurry! So hurry up and hurry!)

Well, that goal is silly. If they actually do accomplish it, their churches will be among the most shallow churches in history. Any man who would even *think* such a thought as ten thousand churches in ten years has *utterly* underestimated the fall of man, the weakness of man, the depravity of man, the rebelliousness of man, the independence of man, *and* God's need for time to transform the individual soul.

But most of all he does not understand man's inhumanity to man. Especially when men are religious! You will see fights, splits, immorality, dictatorship, conformity, fear, more splits, scoundrels, and, in general, the terrorizing of God's people. Not to mention that the whole idea of growth that fast has not a shred of scriptural witness.

When those ten years are up, you won't have ten thousand churches, but you will have spiritual corpses strewn all over a bloody battlefield. And don't forget, you will have some of the most shallow, *fantasizing* churches on God's good earth.

Later we will compare this movement mentality and goal-setting mentality to that of the greatest church planter of all times, one Paul of Tarsus!

But what has a movement mentality got to do with unity in the body of Christ?

Movements preclude unity.

To illustrate. Two movements—both new—find themselves in the same city. Will they come together? That is an impossibility. Each of those two movements is driven by a vast vision. The vision is the *source* of their power. Each movement is also unified and cohesive only because of their vision. That vision is the motor, power, direction and purpose of the movement. Each of the two movements, of course, has a *different* vision. The fatal flaw is obvious. Remove the vision and the movement falls apart.

By the way, both movements will surely claim that Christ is that vision. But Christ is *not* the center of *either* movement. Ask one of them to talk for twenty minutes a day for six months about Christ, without bringing up *any* side subject, or without mentioning this vision. I've got money in my clothes that says he won't last a week... and some of his twenty-minute talks will probably be on *the names of Christ in the Old Testament,* so as to fill up his time slot.

Movements of any kind have no place in the Christian faith, at least not from a scriptural vantage point.

But can the kingdom of God go forth *without* movements? Frankly, I for one am not sure it can go *forward* at all *with* movements.*

---

*Do I hear someone back there on the last pew saying, "You folks trying to have unity will end up with another denomination just like everyone else did."

I challenge that. It is an oft-made statement, but it is a statement full of holes. If *everyone* until this good hour has failed *and* ended up a denomination or a movement, then that only increases the odds for our not failing.

Please note the witness of Paul's life. He did not start (1) a movement, nor (2) did he found a large number of churches.

No, we do not have to fail. We do not have to end up being either another movement nor another denomination. In fact, we will *not* be. (Doubter, please read on.) But if fail we must, then brother, hear me: I for one want to be caught failing while going for that which is closest to the heart of God... *His bride.* I'd rather fail at that than succeed at lesser things.

And if the cause be hopeless, then did you not know:

*A hopeless cause is the*
*only cause worth fighting for.*

The following thoughts will probably be new to you. I hope they will be arresting to you.

Paul of Tarsus never launched a movement.

Paul was a traveling (wandering) church planter. He planted churches and then moved on. He came back to visit and "shore up" those churches, but only occasionally.

Furthermore, Paul was *not* a full-time Christian worker. He was not a part-time Christian worker. He earned his own living. Paul *worked for a living*. The greatest church planter of all times planted churches *in his spare time*.

In his *spare* time!

(This fellow obviously did not know that the hour was late, that the time was short, that the present world conditions called for men to "burn out" for God, that the world was going to hell in a paper sack, and that the Lord was coming back any minute now, and we had all better be out there winning souls. If he had known that, he surely would have at least quit his job and "raised his support" so he could go full time.)

"But isn't he the man who turned the world upside down?"

Acts 17:6 not withstanding, no he did not.

Here are the facts: In his lifetime Paul planted no more than fifteen churches. (Pushed to its absolute limits, you *might* come up with twenty!)

Twenty churches in one lifetime? Raised up by a wanderer who worked for a living and who did God's work in his spare time!

This is *not* the impression we have of what a Christian worker is!

Twenty churches—a movement?

Furthermore that handful of churches Paul did raise up kept him as busy as a one-legged football player! Those *few* churches drove him crazy, drained his energy, broke his heart, ruined his health, and nearly killed him outright.

And you want ten thousand churches in ten years? Where will you get five hundred Pauls?! It would take you a generation to raise up just two or three such men...with all the breaks falling in your favor. And another lifetime for those two or three *or four* men to raise up fifteen or twenty churches. That's a total of sixty to eighty churches in one life span!

Any worker who thinks in terms of raising up over fifteen or twenty churches in his lifetime needs to be locked up. He is a menace to Christian society! For sure, he knows nothing of the difficulties involved in raising up a real experience of church life.

None of us will *ever* do a better work than Paul, and his limit was *twenty churches in one lifetime!*

Stick with *that* standard and you will never see another movement. *Never!*

Raise up five hundred or a thousand churches and there is good reason to believe you have never even *seen* what the church of Jesus Christ really is. And what you would have when you finished *probably* would not even qualify to be called *ecclesia*.

God give us Christian workers—a new breed of church planters—bent on *not* being a movement.

No, if itinerate men spend a lifetime raising up twenty churches, *there will be no movement!* And that day, and those men, *will* come.

* * *

Now let's ask a really central question about Paul's churches.

Would Baptists and Methodists *both* be allowed in one of the churches Paul raised up? Wow! What a question. Would Luther, Zwingli, Calvin *and* an Anabaptist all get in?

Could a pre-, a post-, and an amillennialist *all* get in? Could those who are interested (and those *not* interested) in evangelism, healing, miracles, prophesies, counseling, baptism, tongues, the Lord's supper, the second coming, family life, home schooling, and vegetables...could *all* these people be received in churches raised up by Paul?

Yes!

Why?

Because the centrality of Paul's ministry was Christ. Even circumcising, legalistic, narrow-minded Judaizers got in!!

And if Paul found out another church planter had raised up a church in the same place he had planted one, would they have come together?

Yes!

Why? *Because it would not affect Paul's income nor his position!*

And *this* is the kind of worker the future needs so desperately. Men who are broken. Men who are itinerate (non-local). Men who work for a living. Men who are centered on nothing but Christ. Men who stay clear of doctrines of "doubtful disputation." Men who do *not* launch movements, but give their whole lives to the raising up (and perfecting) the body of Christ in a few locales. In one lifetime—in only a *few* cities. Men who do not network those twenty churches into a structure with other church planters in other cities. Men who can surrender their work and their income, their positions and their pride, to the greater purpose of unity in the body of Christ, anywhere, anytime.

Dear reader, this is the kind of worker we need in order to see the beginning of unity among simple believers in the body of Christ. May the story of church history one day be dominated by such Christian workers.

Accept no substitutes.

Are *you* ready for such men to appear?

# 30
# Are You Ready for Unity?

The following people are all about to sell their homes and move to Centraltown, U.S.A. for the purpose of joining with and having church life with a group of Christians who are already meeting in Centraltown. You are one of the people involved. You just arrived. Let's take a look at all those other people you will soon be meeting with.

One of the people you will meet with is a devout *pre*-millennialist. Another is a *post-*, and another is an *a*millennialist. There is also a fire-breathing evangelist in the group; another brother who is a door-to-door soul winner; another brother—who just arrived today—had his whole life transformed by "receiving the Baptism, with tongues following!" Another has been teaching home Bible classes all over America for thirty-five years. (He can prove tongues is of the devil, by the way.)

There is also a man in this group who is into prophesying; he is already telling stories about prophecies concerning Jerusalem, Persia, Babylon, etc. He and another fellow are also into healing. ("God's power needs to be seen in the church.")

Then there is the fellow who is into counseling. ("I can tell that no one here is in touch with the secret motives of his heart.") But, boy, *he* can see the secret motives of *everyone's* hearts...especially the leaders. This man feels everyone present has some great needs and should be in counseling...and relationships. ("The church is nothing but relationships. We need this to be emphasized or there *is* surely going to be a split someday.") He's probably right, too...split by him if he doesn't get his way.

Then there is the couple into health foods, and someone else who is into home schooling.

And then there is this truly mind-boggling thing of Christians adopting Old Testament songs, dances, customs, dress, *and* even rituals. Lots of folks are into this!

God alone knows what's cooking in the minds of the rest of those sitting there in the living room on the first day of church life in Centraltown. But there is one guy over there who has already mentioned fifteen times that he is an elder. His friend is into "recovering the five-fold gifts."

Can this church survive?

I leave you to answer that question.

* * *

I would like a word with each of you there in Centraltown. I'll start with those of you who are into schemes of eschatology.

Those of you who are "pre's": Until now you've lived your whole Christian life in a world where *everyone* is a "pre." Daniel, Ezekiel, Revelation, the beast, dragon toes, horns, and a fellow named *Triple Six* are your daily fare. You can hardly think in terms of people *not* believing in premillennianism.

Just a minute. Did you know that half the *evangelical* ministers in America are *not* "pre's"? Can *you* live with non-pre's?

You know all about "a's," you say. (You read about them in books written by "pre's.") You know "a's" are liberals, never evangelistic, aren't big on missions, have no scriptural grounds for existing, etc.

Please go on believing in premillennianism, but please don't push it. It is *still* a *minority* view; there are other Christians who do not believe the premillennial theory.

By the way, Southwestern Baptist Seminary has put out more evangelists and missionaries than any other institute in Christian history. It is also amillennial. (How do I know? I'm an alumnus.)

To the fellow who "got the baptism." You are aware, I trust, that some people do not believe in a "second blessing," but believe that all things come at salvation, that the baptism of the Holy Spirit was a baptism of the church and was not an individual matter, and was fulfilled at the celebration of the Feast of Pentecost in 30 A.D. Go on with your beliefs. But remember: Yours is also a minority view.

In fact, that is the exciting thing about peripheral doctrines: There are so many views about each doctrine that *no one* belongs to a group with a *majority* view!

By the way, I belonged to a gathering of believers for eleven years in which tongues was never mentioned. Yet one night I asked everyone present to close their eyes and, if any were present who spoke in tongues, would they please raise their hands. I never, until now, revealed the results of that poll: Half of the people present in that room that night raised their hands! The point is, the subject was never discussed. *And* there was never a word of disagreement *ever* heard on this subject, ever. Not by anyone! Ever!

Those of you who are into prophecy, healing, signs and wonders, can you accept that most of us are here for Christ? Can you pull in your enthusiasm for such things? At least don't push!

"But they are at the very center of Scripture; they are part of the five-fold ministry listed in Ephesians."

Did you know there are *some* believers (please pray for them) who *don't* believe in the five-fold ministry mentioned in Ephesians?

I am one of them!! At last count I was up to seventeen ministries, not five! And personally I think *gifts* have pushed the Lord Jesus (and the church) clean off the stage. Can you bear that? I can live with you. Can you live with me?

To the health-fooders and home-schoolers: Did you know that the people with the fewest Scriptures to back up their views are the most fanatical?

Here is my point: No matter what we believe about *anything* which is mentioned in this chapter:

1. *Everyone of us* holds a *minority* view!
2. All of these subjects, when emphasized, displace Christ as our centrality.

Every person who walks through the living room door there in Centraltown, U.S.A. comes with preconceptions. He has a hard time understanding that *his* preconceptions are a minority view. He is shocked to find there are those present who have strong convictions on this subject that go in the opposite direction from his own.

Can all of us realize we *all* have a minority view in peripheral doctrines? (Nobody has a *majority* view!) I hope so. If so, please back off from pushing your views.

And what of those of you who *really* see that the church's number one job is to win souls! Such people cannot conceptualize any other view.

But there is another view! Try this on for size: The church meets to fulfill God's *eternal* purpose. If the purpose is eternal, then it is a purpose that preceded the fall and extends *beyond* the age of the fall. God's *primary* purpose in creation cannot be to save men. The fact is simple: Man lived on the earth *before* he was lost; therefore, God must have a purpose for man other than redemption from the fall.

Point: Despite your absolute conviction that "*this* is absolutely essential," there *are other views*. Can you give ground to the possibility that your pet idea, *your* all-consuming fire, is not and will not be shared by all the believers gathered in Centraltown?

Now, there is one last member of the fellowship in Centraltown I would like to speak to. It is you, dear reader!

What is your hobby horse? (What do you ride the most?) Can you lay it at the feet of Jesus Christ, who is our *only* centrality? Can you say, "Lord, I really believe in this (the seven dispensations of creation, and that we are in the 'parenthetical age' of the church), but I will not believe in it so strongly that I push others... that I draw others to my belief... that I divide Your very body."

If you can bring the peripheral things to Christ, if you can swallow hard and live with others whose "doubtful disputations" differ from your "doubtful disputations," you are a candidate for experiencing church life with *all* fellow believers.

If not? Go meet in your little igloo with your little band of like-minded doctrinarians! And know that the god of doctrine is more important to you than the body of Christ.

Now to some guidelines... but they are only for those of you who don't find an igloo appealing.

# 31
# Unity...Getting There

May I offer a credo for all of us. It is not my own, but a reflective guideline from many of God's choicest saints. These guidelines are given in the context of a child of God seeking to live out, practically, the experience of the church.

Also, thrown in free, you will find a few guidelines for a Christian worker in the super-impossible situation in which he finds himself while he seeks to relate to other Christian workers who *do* denominate themselves.

## Christian to Christian

I will build no barriers between myself and another believer. Because God accepts him, I accept him...whole heartedly.

Any feelings I might have about being superior to any other believer in *any* way, I will take to the cross.

At the very minimum, as I look at this matter in a practical way, I will accept another brother to the extent he will allow me to accept him. I realize that the practical aspect of this is limited by the limitations he may place on me, but I accept *him* fully. But my acceptance reaches beyond that.

The boundaries of our practical fellowship with one

another extend out to that point where he demands I accept his doctrinal distinctions and conform to his vision, his teachings, his mind-set. I stop there, but I stop for only *one* reason. If I accept all the demands he makes of me—in order that I may be fully received by him—I am cutting myself off from fellowship with *other* believers who do not share his views. He has demanded I limit my fellowship to those like-minded with him; my fellowship with him extends only up to the point where his demands would limit my acceptance of other believers.

I accept a fundamentalist and a Pentecostal. They may down one another, but I accept both. The only limitation I place is a practical one... asking that they not limit me by insisting I accept one of their views and exclude the other, thereby cutting me off from unhindered fellowship with the other!

I will accept any believer into the fellowship of the body of Christ, asking that he accept others in the body of Christ just as he has been accepted by Christ Himself.

* * *

I would add this word: *Please* don't wander in and out of the fellowship of the body of Christ. We are here for Christ and His church. Your long-term *lack* of commitment to the ecclesia causes great damage to the body. I would not ask that you commit yourself to this particular expression of the body of believers, but that a commitment be made to a body of believers *somewhere*.

Next, I acknowledge two things which I do not like, but cannot help.

*First,* the body of Christ is not practicing oneness. There are factions and cliques. I accept that sad fact and try to accept, work with, and fellowship with believers who do not see the need of oneness in His body. I will seek to continue to accept those who are not interested in oneness. I will strive to be one, even with those who insist that oneness be achieved by adhering to *their* movement or doctrines. (I will not accept their exclusionary doctrines, which exclude me from other believers.)

*Secondly,* despite the existing lack of unity, I will live with believers, and be part of a body of believers, and conduct myself within that body of believers *as though all the church—and* all the believers in my area—*were all one and all gathered as one.*

I recognize the two statements made above are *impossible* to reconcile, but I will be caught trying to do both at once!

Who will I not fellowship with? (1) Anyone presently encouraging immorality in the church, and (2) anyone who is committing adultery and who will not stop committing adultery but who insists on still gathering with the same body of believers I am in.

There is a third.

I will stay at arm's length with anyone who has split a body of believers, until (1) he deals with the thing in his heart that made him feel his conviction about some point was important enough to dismember Christ's own body, and (2) he has repented and/or tried, at least, to make restitution for causing that split. (So far, I've not met many people who have split a church who are interested in doing anything mentioned in this paragraph.)

Now, what of my part in unity as it has to do with other Christian workers?

## Worker to Worker

Let us say the place is Anycity, U.S.A. A church has been planted in that city. A fellowship of believers is meeting in a home located in that city. It is discovered that another Christian worker of like spirit has also raised up a church in that same city. Will these two fellowships merge and become one?

If *one* of those groups belongs to a movement, or if it

uses unity as a gimmick to grow, I would hope *not*—no more than I would hope to see the fellowship I met with join a denomination.

If both groups are sincere in desiring a genuine oneness, what steps should be taken? If I were the worker responsible for the birth of one of those groups, what would I do? I would urge the fellowship with which I am related to become one with the others. But I would also urge the following:

(1) That both of the workers responsible for the birth of these two groups cease receiving any money from the two groups!

(2) That all eldership (or any other kind of leadership) in *both* groups be totally *dissolved*. Why? So that *all* the saints in both groups can begin again—together—on equal footing. (This might also help some leaders to discover they were addicted to their leadership role and their title.)

(3) That the newly combined church be left alone by *both* founding workers for at least eighteen months. That is, for both of us to remove ourselves *completely* from the scene so that the two groups truly merge... in spirit... with no outside pressure or manipulation from the two church planters.

And after eighteen months? Let the church decide what it wants to do with the two of us!

And if a split—or conflict—arises in the fellowship that has to do with differences between these two workers?

Well, as soon as I find enough sense to figure out that I am part of the problem and that no reasonable remedy is at hand, I will surrender my work. I *will* depart. I will utterly disengage myself from that church (or any church) when the conflict is over *the worker*.

The church *always* comes before the worker. *Always!*

* * *

As you and I close out this book, I urge you to join

with me in praying for a new breed of workers. Specifically, the re-emergence of a particular... lost... office of the church: the office of *church planter*. And may those men, when they come, be exemplary in their conduct with God's people and place the unity of the body of Christ above all else. And may their message be the centrality of Jesus Christ in *all* things!

But what of the *non*-worker? I urge you to depart from all places that divide over doctrine. Join with those who do not sector themselves off over doctrine. (That is, seriously consider giving up Curse Number Two!)

And may your actions influence others, until simple believers across this planet forsake division based on differences of peripheral doctrines and *minority* views.

Let us circumvent the curse of Constantine (Curse Number One—the invention of divisive doctrines and the demand of doctrinal unity). And let us forsake Curse Number Two (He who has the best theology is best loved and best blessed by a theological God).

Let us hope for the day when men who are doctrinarians and expounders of doubtful disputations look up, only to find none of us are present. And let us look to that day when God raises up a new breed of workers! And laymen who give up doctrinal differences for Lent!

Lord, haste the day!

This book is about church unity and how to get there. We have seen the problems; but those problems belong to the past, to other peoples and to other generations. You and I are alive *today*. In God's eyes you and I are not responsible for the past nor are we responsible for some far distant future. We are responsible for that which occurs *in our lifetime*. It is given to us—and expected of us—to be faithful during our lifetime. Let's get back to unity.

# Supplementary Reading

Let's Return to Christian Unity (Kurosaki)
Our Mission (Edwards)
Preventing a Church Split (Edwards)
Concerning Our Missions (Nee)
Torch of the Testimony (Kennedy)
Love Covers (Bilheimer)

# Order Form

***Church Life***

Revolution
The Story of the Early Church ................. $ 7.95
Preventing a Church Split ..........................hb 6.95
Our Mission .................................................. 8.95
When the Church Was Young .......................... 7.95
Going to Church in the First Century ............. 5.95
The Torch of the Testimony ............................ 8.95
Passing of the Torch ...................................... 7.95
Let's Return to Christian Unity ........................ 6.95
Church Unity...How to Get There ................ 6.95
Church Life Before Constantine .................... 19.95

***The Deeper Christian Life***

The Highest Life ........................................... 7.95
The Secret to the Christian Life ...................... 7.95
Experiencing the Depths of Jesus Christ .......... 7.95
Practicing His Presence ................................. 7.95
The Spiritual Guide ....................................... 7.95
Final Steps in Christian Maturity .................... 7.95
Spiritual Torrents .......................................... 7.95
Guyon Speaks Again ..................................... 7.95
Fenelon's Spiritual Letters ............................. 7.95

***Brokenness***

A Tale of Three Kings ................................... 6.95
The Prisoner in the Third Cell ....................... 7.95
The Inward Journey ....................................... 7.95
Letters to a Devastated Christian .................... 4.95

***Death and Consolation***

Dear Lillian .................................................. 5.95

***Inspiration***

The Divine Romance ..................................... 7.95
Turkeys and Eagles ....................................... 6.95

***Evangelism***

You Can Witness with Confidence .................. 7.95

***Other Books by Jeanne Guyon***

The Song of the Bride ................................... 9.95
Union with God ............................................. 6.95
Genesis ........................................................ 9.95
The Way Out (Exodus) ................................. 9.95

* * *

**Christian Books Publishing House**
**P.O. Box 3368**
**Auburn, Maine 04212-3368**